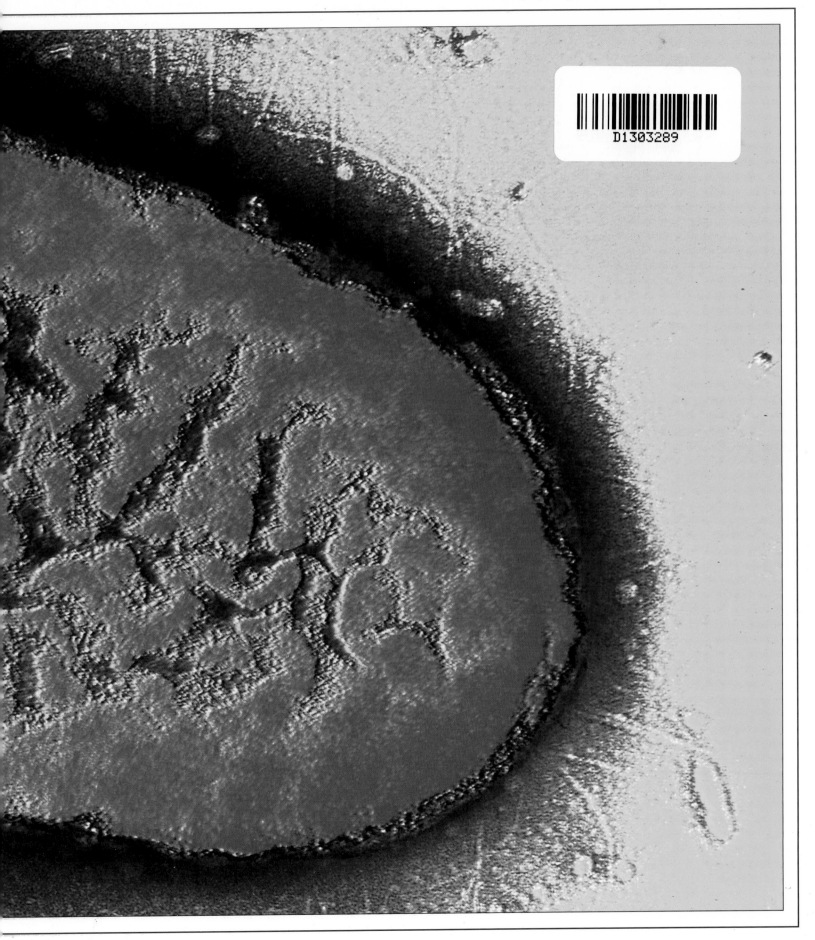

The whooping cough bacterium magnified over 30,000 times.

7/19

HUMAN BODY

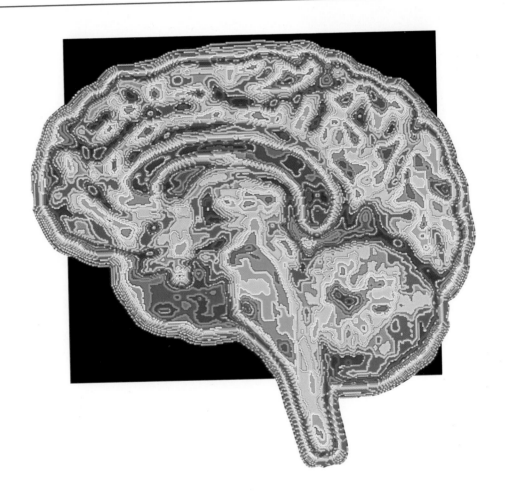

A computer-generated image of the human brain.

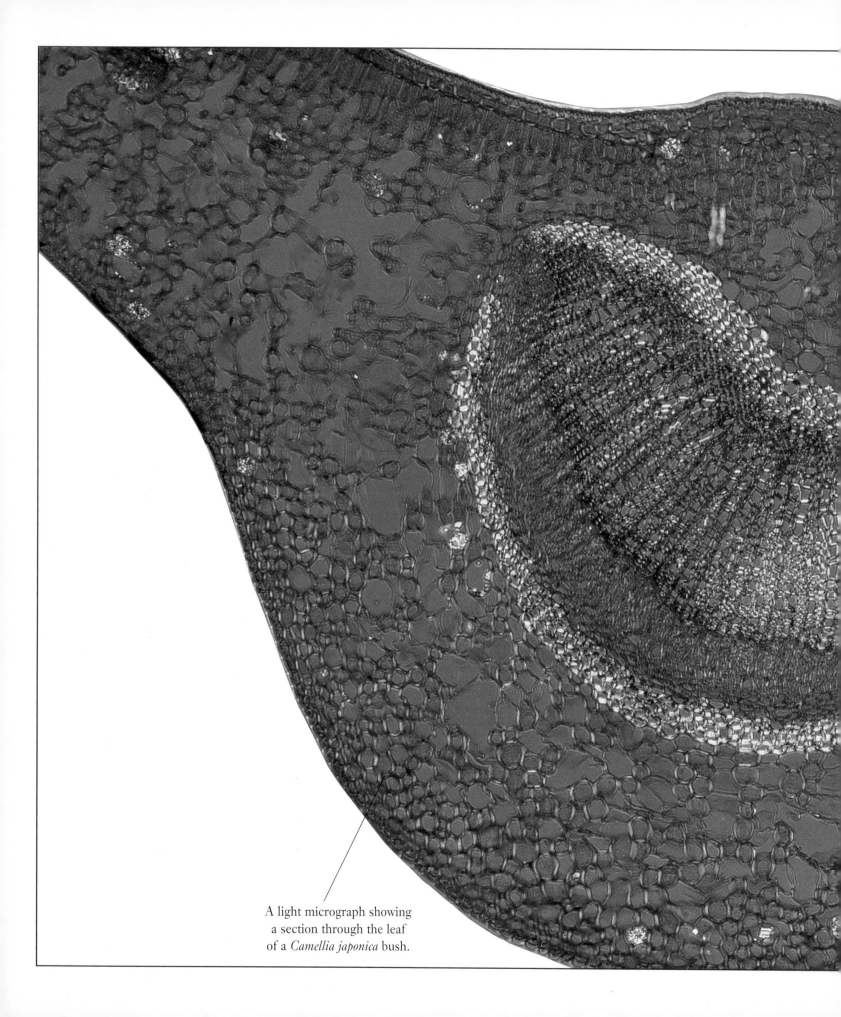

A light micrograph showing
a section through the leaf
of a *Camellia japonica* bush.

SCIENCE FACTS

HUMAN BODY

LIONEL BENDER

CRESCENT BOOKS
NEW YORK • AVENEL, NEW JERSEY

CLB 2753

© 1992 Colour Library Books Ltd., Godalming, Surrey, England

This 1992 edition published by Crescent Books,
distributed by Outlet Book Company, Inc.,
a Random House Company
40 Engelhard Avenue, Avenel, New Jersey 07001

Printed and bound in Italy

ISBN 0 517 06554 1

8 7 6 5 4 3 2 1

The Author
Lionel Bender is a writer and editor with nearly 20 years of experience of
producing illustrated information books for adults and children, mostly in the
fields of science and natural history. He has an honors degree in Biological
Sciences from Birmingham University, England, and is a Scientific Fellow of
the Zoological Society of London. He has written more than 35 books
himself, and, as a director of Lionheart Books and Bender Richardson
White, has edited and produced even more than this for the international
book market.

Credits
Editor: Philip de Ste. Croix
Designers: Stonecastle Graphics Ltd.
Color artwork: Rod Ferring © Colour Library Books Ltd.
Picture Editor: Miriam Sharland
Production: Ruth Arthur, Sally Connolly, Andrew Whitelaw
Director of Production: Gerald Hughes
Typesetting: SX Composing Ltd.
Printed and bound by New Interlitho SpA, Italy

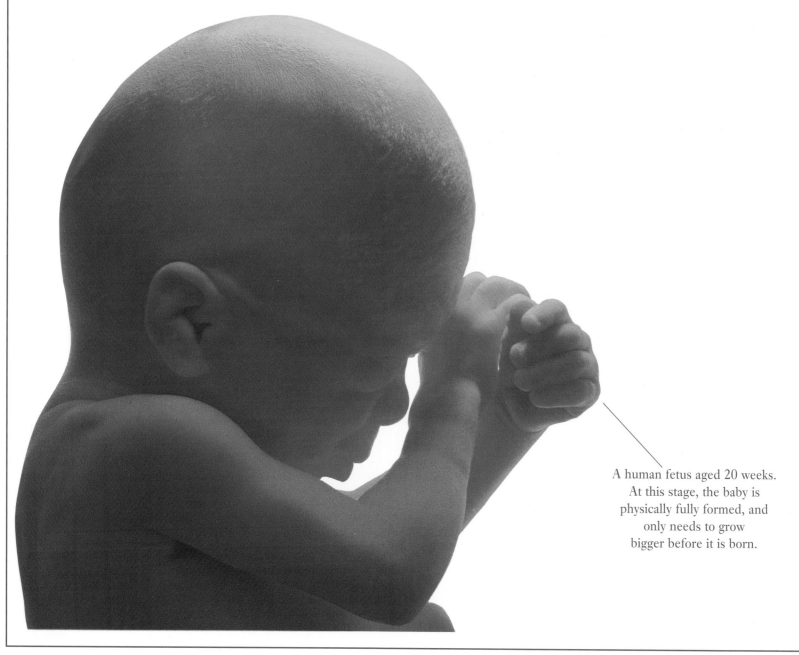

A human fetus aged 20 weeks.
At this stage, the baby is
physically fully formed, and
only needs to grow
bigger before it is born.

CONTENTS

Different bodies, the same wonders

As we shall see, the human body is far more complex than any machine, and has reasoning abilities greater than those of any computer. Yet how it works is still not fully understood. We know much about its structure and form, and what it can do, but many of its activities read more like science fiction than science fact.

The same is true of our fellow animals, and of plants and other living creatures, which include fungi, algae such as seaweeds, and bacteria. Fascination with and scientific investigation of living things dates back to ancient times. By around 1700 B.C. the Egyptians were writing – in picture and sign form – about organs of the body such as the stomach, bladder, and heart, and how they seemed to interrelate. Their knowledge came mainly from preparing the dead – cats, dogs, and birds as well as people –

for mummification (a way of preserving a body by embalming it) and life in the next world. This involved removing the brain, lungs, and stomach, and treating the rest of the body with chemicals.

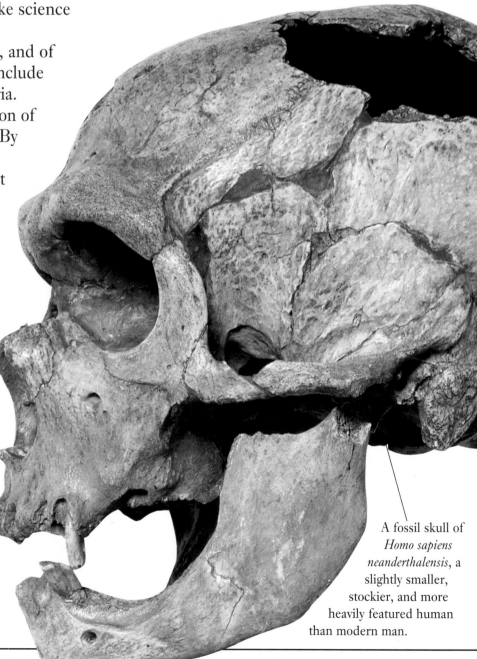

To this artist, the mechanisms of the mind conjure up images of electronic circuits, and the realm of computers.

A fossil skull of *Homo sapiens neanderthalensis*, a slightly smaller, stockier, and more heavily featured human than modern man.

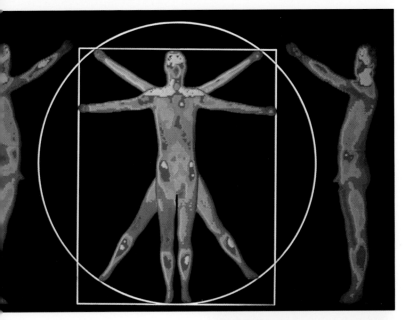

the microscope was invented. The detailed anatomy of all living things, or organisms, could now be examined. It was soon realized that all creatures are made up of similar components that work in almost identical ways. They all have parts for processing food, for transporting materials around their structure, for getting rid of wastes, and so on. Therefore, the term 'body' justifiably can be used with reference to any living thing.

Evolution has created more than 10 million different kinds, or species, of organisms, each adapted to a particular environment and way of life. As we will also show, each reveals a number of remarkable bodily attributes.

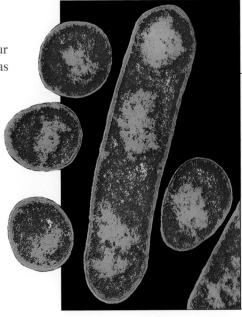

The brain capacity of Neanderthal man was similar to our own. Speech was possible.

These are bacteria seen at x14,000 magnification using an electron microscope. This instrument has revealed a similarity in structure among living things down to the molecular level.

Today, with the help of X-ray machines and scanners, we can study the anatomy of living things without having to dissect them, as in this scan of a section through the human head.

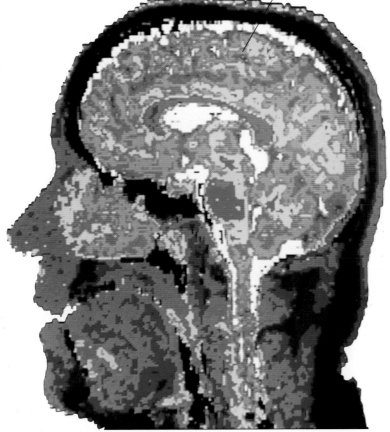

In Europe, during the 15th to 17th centuries A.D., there was a 'rebirth' or renaissance in arts and sciences. This was the time of great scientists and philosophers such as Galileo, Leonardo da Vinci, and René Descartes. Among them was Andreas Vesalius (1514-1564), a Belgian physician who revolutionized human anatomy, the study of the structure of our bodies. He cut up human cadavers to examine the arrangement of muscles, bones, and blood vessels. This practice had been banned for centuries on religious grounds. In 1590,

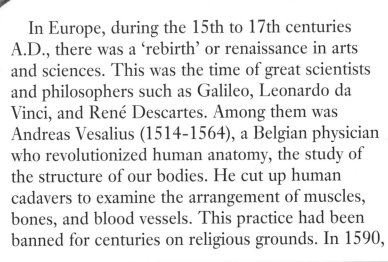

Living and non-living

As long ago as the 4th century B.C., the Greek philosopher and scientist Aristotle noted that the body is more than a machine – it has a life force. Almost 2,000 years later, William Shakespeare, in his play *Hamlet*, wrote: 'What a piece of work is a man! How noble in reason! how infinite in faculty! in form, in moving, how express and admirable! in action how like an angel! in apprehension how like a god! the beauty of the world! the paragon of animals! And yet, to me, what is this quintessence of dust?'

Clearly, Shakespeare thought of the human being as the perfect and most advanced of creatures. But not every educated person of the time felt the same. In the 17th century, the English satirical writer Samuel Butler once described the human body as 'a pair of pincers set over a bellows and a stewpan and the whole thing fixed upon stilts.' It was only in the mid-19th century that scientists finally established the unique features of living things and formulated our present ideas about how life on Earth evolved.

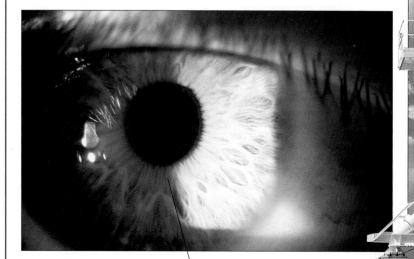

The human eye – our window on the world and a model for every camera design. The iris contracts and dilates to admit light, rather like a camera's shutter.

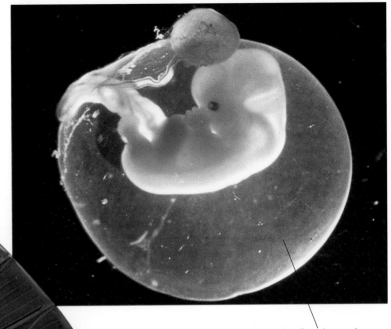

A human embryo at about 6 weeks. Limbs and a head region are evident, but recognition as an independent living being is still many weeks away.

Picking up an object with fingers. Not a human hand, but that of a robot – an inanimate being but nevertheless capable of animated movement.

So what are the differences between living and non-living – animate and inanimate – things? Or, as the popular biology exam question asks, 'What are the differences between an *Amoeba* (a tiny pond animal) and a motor car?' There are just seven main differences – living things respire, excrete, feed, move, are sensitive to their surroundings, grow, and reproduce. In this book we shall look at each of these in turn and show that while some machines have been designed to achieve one or more of these abilities – a car to move and a camera to respond to light, for instance – none can perform them all. A mouse may see, smell, or hear a cat that is about to pounce on it and scurry away into its hole, but a car about to collide with another does not have an in-built escape system. However, we shall be drawing analogies between animate and inanimate objects so you can make these comparisons and contrasts for yourself.

A mother giraffe and her offspring. Reproduction of the species is the greatest of all abilities of living things. (An oxpecker bird is removing parasites from the mother's skin.)

Life force

The distinction between living and non-living things is not always so clear. Viruses, for instance, which cause such human diseases as poliomyelitis, AIDS, and influenza, can live and reproduce only within living animals, plants, or bacteria. Outside such an environment, they are inanimate clusters of chemicals. Some can be made into crystals like sugar and salt.

Then there is the question of when is a living thing dead? What happens when the life force leaves the body? For ourselves, the obvious signs of death are when movement ceases, when breathing stops, and the heart does not beat for a few minutes. Medically, though, it is defined as when there is also no electrical activity in the brain. Much the same criteria (or rules) are used for other animals. But with plants, bacteria, and viruses, the same values do not apply. Some of these creatures can remain dormant for months, years, or even millennia. They seem dead but then, when conditions are right, they suddenly burst into life. Scientists look for signs of

Three generations – grandparents, parent, and child. There is an African saying, 'No condition is permanent.' Everything changes with time. We are born, we grow up, age, and die. We are not yet able to change the natural history of human life.

A pupa stage of the Small tortoiseshell butterfly. It appears dormant, almost lifeless, but inside, the caterpillar's body is being transformed into the winged adult.

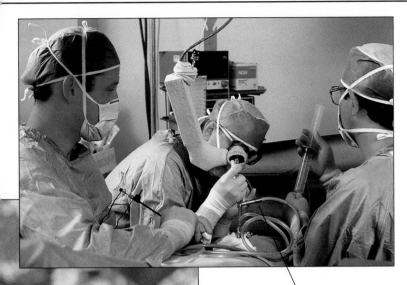

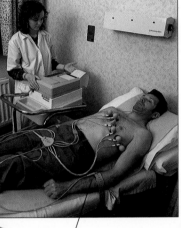

life in these creatures by detecting whether or not they are performing various aspects of their normal chemistry – breaking down food to release energy or getting rid of wastes – or whether they are growing or reproducing or can be made to do so. Criteria such as these can be used to determine life or death in any type of creature.

Another puzzle of life remains. What causes ageing? Why do all living things eventually die? Almost from the day we are born, parts of our bodies start to die. Nerve cells, for example, die and are not replaced, while skin and muscle cells continue to grow and reproduce. Why is this? Would it be possible to slow down and stop the ageing process? Scientists have now explained most living processes in terms of chemical reactions, and can even produce the basic substances of living things in the laboratory. But like the medieval alchemists who tried to make gold from iron, biologists have still not succeeded in isolating the life force and creating living things artificially.

Manipulating nature – a surgeon removes eggs from a woman's ovary for fertilization in a test-tube. Any embryo that forms will then be implanted in her uterus.

Modern medicine, like this ECG examination of the heart, is prolonging the human lifespan – now, in the West, by a year or two each decade.

Not an abstract painting but muscle fibers, living tissue from the human body. Muscle action involves molecular changes within cells powered by energy derived from food.

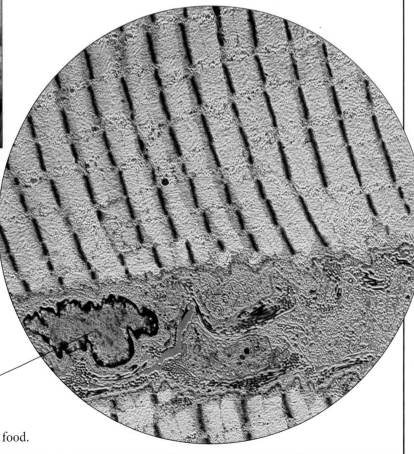

The building bricks of life

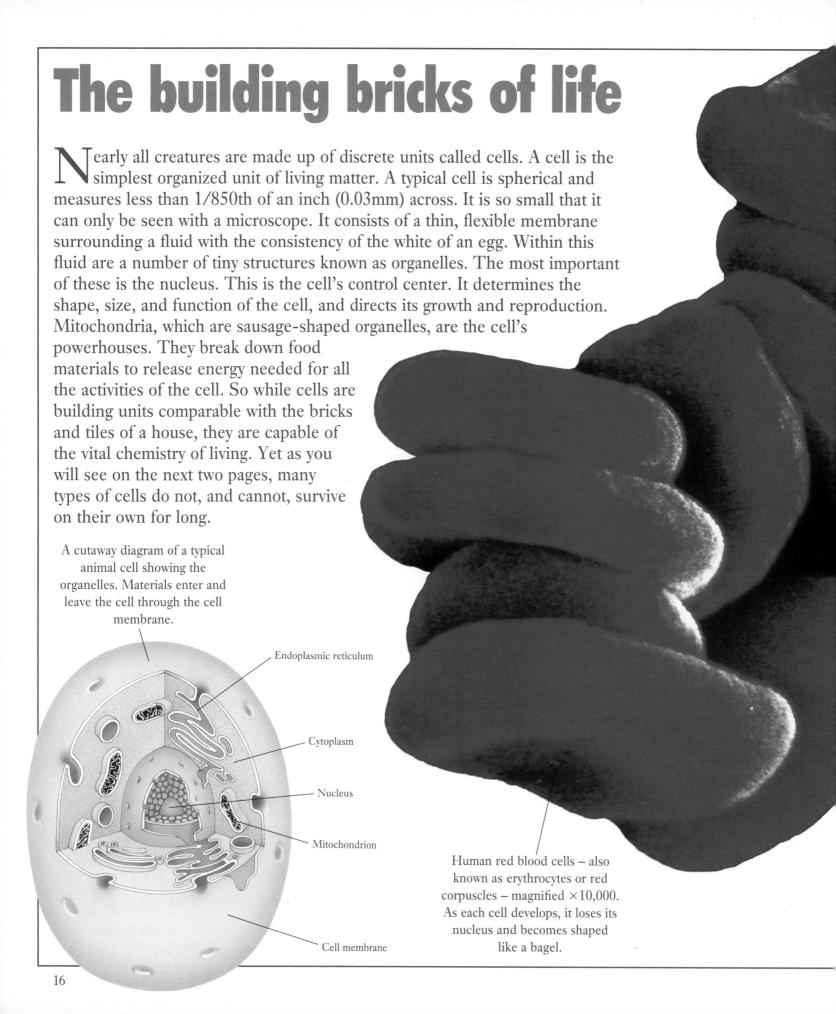

Nearly all creatures are made up of discrete units called cells. A cell is the simplest organized unit of living matter. A typical cell is spherical and measures less than 1/850th of an inch (0.03mm) across. It is so small that it can only be seen with a microscope. It consists of a thin, flexible membrane surrounding a fluid with the consistency of the white of an egg. Within this fluid are a number of tiny structures known as organelles. The most important of these is the nucleus. This is the cell's control center. It determines the shape, size, and function of the cell, and directs its growth and reproduction. Mitochondria, which are sausage-shaped organelles, are the cell's powerhouses. They break down food materials to release energy needed for all the activities of the cell. So while cells are building units comparable with the bricks and tiles of a house, they are capable of the vital chemistry of living. Yet as you will see on the next two pages, many types of cells do not, and cannot, survive on their own for long.

A cutaway diagram of a typical animal cell showing the organelles. Materials enter and leave the cell through the cell membrane.

Endoplasmic reticulum

Cytoplasm

Nucleus

Mitochondrion

Cell membrane

Human red blood cells – also known as erythrocytes or red corpuscles – magnified ×10,000. As each cell develops, it loses its nucleus and becomes shaped like a bagel.

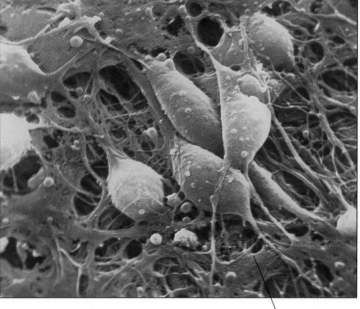

The pigment hemoglobin, which gives erythrocytes their red color, combines with oxygen from air breathed in by the lungs.

Nerve cells from the human brain, each with a nucleus contained in a central cell body (stained yellow-green) and with many thin projections.

Plant cells, with shared cell walls and many air-filled spaces or vacuoles. The darkly stained spheres visible here are the cell nuclei.

The inner lining of our breathing tubes. It contains mucus-secreting cells and cells with hairs that beat to keep out bacteria and dust.

❑ The human body is made up of more than 10 million million cells. The largest is the woman's ovum or egg. It measures nearly 1/250th of an inch (0.1mm) in diameter, a little smaller than a pinhead.

❑ The largest cell of all is the ostrich's egg. It is approximately 7in long and 5½in across (178 × 140mm) – only a little smaller than an American football.

❑ Live bacterial cells more than 1,500 years old have been found in mud samples taken from the bottom of lakes.

❑ The tiny water creature *Euglena gracilis* consists of a single cell that has both animal and plant characteristics. It can move and is highly sensitive but, like green plants, it can make its own food.

❑ Bacteria are our distant relatives! It is likely that the mitochondria in our cells are the descendants of bacteria-like organisms that invaded primitive animal cells millions of years ago. The chloroplasts of plant cells – the food-producing units – probably have a similar history.

❑ Bacteria are so small that about 1,000 of them would be needed to cover the period at the end of this sentence.

Levels of organization

Organisms such as a fern, a frog, or an elephant are, like ourselves, made up of millions of cells. Others, like *Amoeba, Euglena*, and bacteria, consist of just one cell. There are, however, no more than about 200 types of cell in the living world. These include nerve, muscle, blood, and liver cells (animals), and root-hair, and water-conducting cells (plants). Within multicellular creatures (organisms made up of many cells), cells are usually arranged in various groups or layers known as tissues, and tissues are grouped together to make functional units called organs. In turn, organs are linked together to make body systems. For example, bone cells, blood-vessel cells, and marrow cells form the major tissues of long bones that, joined together, form the skeletal system. The cells in each tissue work together in a coordinated fashion so that the tissue performs a wider range of functions than any of its constituent parts. In the same way, in football, soccer, or baseball the individual players, coaches, trainers, and manager work together to create a team.

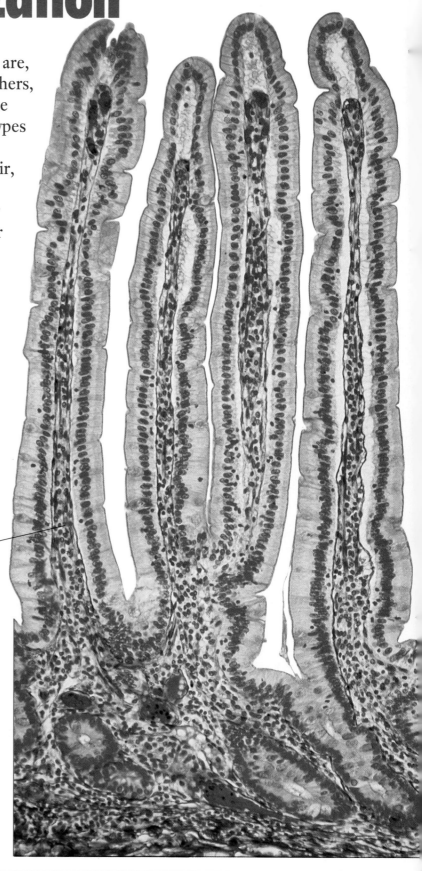

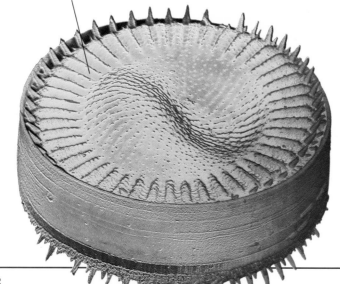

A diatom, a single-celled alga, found in streams and lakes. Its cell wall consists of two glassy shells which fit together like a pillbox.

Millions of multicellular projections only 1/25th of an inch (1mm) long, the villi, form the inner surface of the human small intestine – six villi are seen.

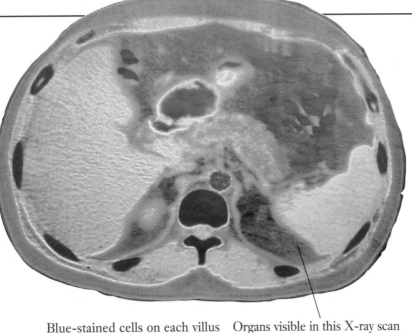

Blue-stained cells on each villus secrete digestive juices, the pink-stained ones absorb nutrients. Blood and lymph vessels extend up the villi.

Organs visible in this X-ray scan through the human abdomen include the liver (yellow, left), pancreas (centre, green), and spleen (yellow, right).

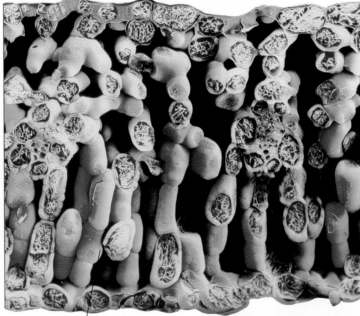

Section through a turnip leaf, with many cells sliced open revealing a spongy interior and thousands of tiny green chloroplasts.

A Snakelocks anemone, a coelenterate, an animal with a body wall only two cell layers thick.

❏ The proportion of different types of cell in the human body changes with age. In the newborn, muscle tissue accounts for about 25 percent by weight, and nerve tissue in the brain about 13 percent. In the adult, the relative proportions are 43 percent and 2 percent by weight respectively.

❏ Catkins are the male reproductive organs of trees such as birches. Each of them can produce more than 5 million pollen grains, the male reproductive cells.

❏ *Wolffia angusta*, an aquatic duckweed from Australia, is the smallest flowering plant in the world. It has the same types of cells, tissues, organs, and body systems as the giants of the plant world, the 260ft- (80m-) tall sequoia and redwood trees of California, but it is only 1/500th of an inch (0.05mm) long and 1/800th of an inch (0.032mm) wide.

❏ We are made up of just three basic layers of cells. In the developing embryo, the outer ectoderm gives rise to skin cells, the nervous system, and sense organs. The middle layer, the mesoderm, produces muscle, bone, blood cells, and many major organs, and the inner endoderm gives rise to the digestive system and its associated organs.

The sphere – nature's most versatile structure

Asphere is the perfect form. From its center, all points on its surface are an equal distance away, it is symmetrical in all planes, and all forces radiating out are evenly spread. In nature, therefore, the sphere as a body form has evolved on many separate occasions. The typical living cell, for example, is spherical, with the nucleus at its center. The spores of fungi, algae, and bacteria are spheres, as are the egg cells of most vertebrates – animals with a backbone – such as ourselves. Indeed, we all started life as a sphere, as a tiny ball of cells formed by division of a fertilized egg. In the physical world, water droplets, soap bubbles, the Sun and planets, all are spheres formed as a result of a balance of forces acting from within and on their surfaces. Acknowledging a sphere's unique characteristics, we have developed the ball for use in sports, and in machines.

A new human being in the making? An ovum, or egg, in the fallopian tube enclosed in a layer of cells that a sperm may penetrate to fertilize it.

A spherical pollen grain, one of the male sex cells of conifers and flowering plants. Pollen is dispersed by wind or by insects when they visit a flower and rub against the stamens that produce it.

The outer wall of this pollen grain has a spiky structure that helps it anchor itself on the stigma, the female part of a flower.

Sphere with a view – nighttime photo of the dome of the 33ft (10m) diameter Keck telescope on the summit of Mauna Kea, Hawaii.

The round face of a dandelion 'clock,' so-called as the number of puffs needed to dislodge all the seeds supposedly gives the hour.

A slice through the fruit of a poppy reveals segments packed with spherical seeds. As the fruit dries, these are released through window-like pores at its top.

Symmetry – patterns in nature

A jellyfish, a sea anemone, and an oak tree have a body plan like a cake cut from the center in V-shaped slices – a number of identical units radiating from a central point. These creatures are said to show radial symmetry. Coccal bacteria, spores, and *Amoeba* can be cut in identical units in all planes from their centers. They show spherical symmetry. A flatworm, a cow, a fish, and a human being have a body plan in which one half is a mirror image of the other half. They display what is called bilateral symmetry. These three patterns of shape and form pervade the living world. In the animal world, the most advanced species – fish, amphibians, mammals like ourselves, and so on – are all bilaterally symmetrical. This is linked to the evolution of a definite head- or front-end, with a brain and sense organs such as eyes and ears. The animal leads with this part of the body as it moves. Interestingly, in the world of computers, a robot – an 'intelligent' machine built to move – is bilaterally symmetrical, whereas a database has a central 'brain' and terminals at the ends of radiating links.

The beauty of symmetry. This woman is sitting in the 'lotus position' for yoga exercises, to create harmony between mind and body.

The Great Pyramids at Giza, Egypt. These were built over 4,000 years ago. With their square bases, they display four-fold symmetry.

A common starfish displaying five-fold symmetry. The arms, which radiate from a central point, bear tube-feet for collecting food and to help the animal cling to surfaces.

Five-fold symmetry deep within a carrion flower, a native of South Africa. The flower's smell attracts insects that normally feed on dung, and these pollinate the flower.

Bacterial cells, like these that cause diseases in humans, reproduce by a symmetrical splitting in two of each cell and its contents.

FACT FILE

❑ The human body is not, on the inside, perfectly symmetrical. There is only one heart, one liver, one stomach and so on, and each of these organs is positioned to one side of the midline.

❑ Starfish have a basic five-fold symmetry – five arms radiating from a central region. But some have 40 arms, and an arm that becomes detached through injury can grow into a new starfish.

❑ Radial symmetry is more common among plants than among animals. There is usually an odd number of segments, as in an orange and tangerine fruit, and in spore- and pollen-producing capsules.

❑ Snowflakes show radial symmetry. Each flake consists of a six-sided plate with branching arms radiating out from the corners of the plate.

❑ Brains are found only in animals with bilateral symmetry.

Food processing – preparing for digestion

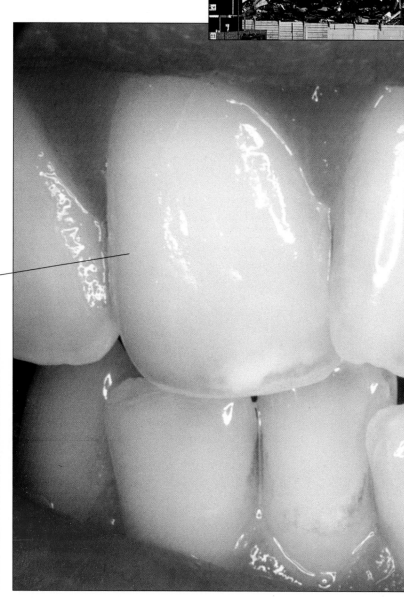

Living things need energy to drive the chemical reactions that keep their bodies fit and healthy. To get this energy, they must feed. Green plants, and some bacteria and algae, make their own food. They use the energy of sunlight to combine the simple chemical compounds, carbon dioxide and water, into complex sugars, or carbohydrates. This process is known as photosynthesis. The sugars are then broken down, or digested, in cells to release the energy. Photosynthesis depends on the possession of pigments able to absorb the radiant energy of the Sun – cholorophyll in green plants and red, brown, or blue pigments called phycobolins in bacteria and algae. All other living things must break down complex chemical compounds into simpler ones to release the bound-up energy. This involves an elaborate food-processing system. The food we eat must be pulverized and liquidized before any energy can be liberated. This starts in the mouth, with both mechanical and chemical attacks on our meal.

An *Amoeba*, in life a creature about the size of a pinhead, puts out a false-foot to engulf a *Paramecium*, another single-celled animal.

Teeth – the first of our food-processing devices. The incisors – the big front teeth – bite and cut food. The neighboring canines bite and tear.

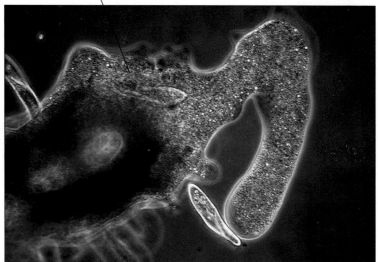

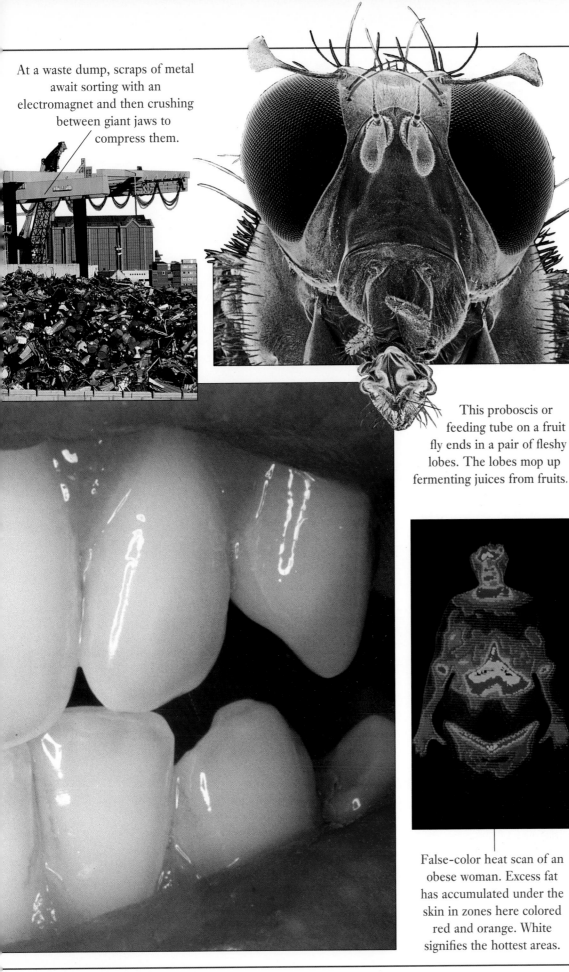

At a waste dump, scraps of metal await sorting with an electromagnet and then crushing between giant jaws to compress them.

This proboscis or feeding tube on a fruit fly ends in a pair of fleshy lobes. The lobes mop up fermenting juices from fruits.

False-color heat scan of an obese woman. Excess fat has accumulated under the skin in zones here colored red and orange. White signifies the hottest areas.

FACT FILE

❑ Frenchman Michel Lotito, popularly known as Monsieur Mangetout (Mr Eat-everything), has the unique ability to eat up to 2lb (900g) of metal and glass each day without ill-effect. He has even apparently consumed a small light aircraft in Caracas, Venezuela. But he must balance his diet with normal amounts of ordinary food, from which he gets all the nourishment he needs.

❑ An adult elephant needs about 300lb (136kg) of plant food a day – as much greenstuff as 2,000 people might eat in a day.

❑ Vampire bats feed on the blood of large mammals, including humans, and may drink more than their own body weight – 1¾oz (50g) – in blood at each meal.

❑ Most human babies are born without teeth, but Julius Caesar, Napoleon Bonaparte, and King Richard III of England are among those who are reputed to have had a single tooth at birth.

❑ Earthworms feed on soil and decaying animal and plant material. They get rid of undigested material as casts. In a plot of land the size of a football field there are millions of earthworms and they can turn over more than 50 tons (45 tonnes) of soil in a year.

Digesting one's meal

Within the large intestine, water and salts are removed from the remains of chemical digestion. The appendix has no function.

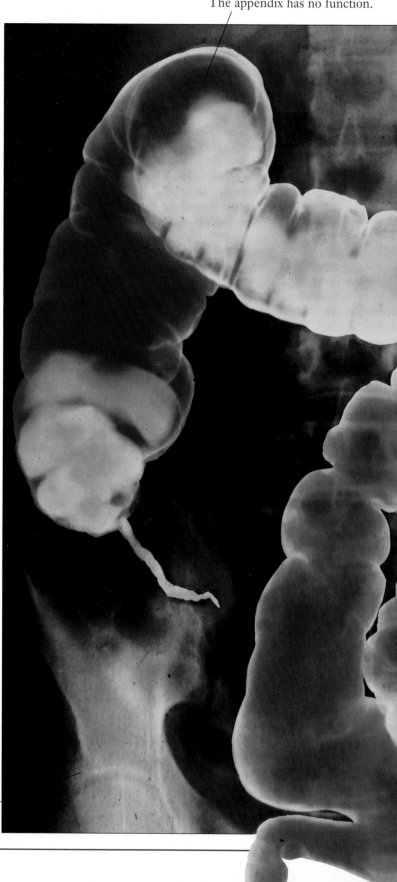

Many fungi live on a diet of dead or decaying material, such as animal dung and carcasses, rotting wood and fruit, and humus. Houseflies have a similar diet. These organisms are not equipped to eat solid food materials, as we are, but only liquids. Fungi release a cocktail of chemicals that break down complex foods into simple substances, which are absorbed through their cell walls. Houseflies spread digestive juices over their food to create a nutrient liquid, which they then suck up. The majority of animals ingest solid foods, but quickly break these down to form a thick, creamy 'broth.' However the nutrient liquid is made, it is then subjected to attack by special chemicals known as enzymes. These are nature's catalysts or chemical helpers. They direct and control the speed of chemical processes in the body, and can be used over and over again. To digest a meal, perhaps 100 different enzymes are involved. One small step at a time, they break down the major constituents of food – carbohydrates, fats, and proteins – into forms of nutrient that individual cells can utilize.

A man-made chemical plant, where liquid materials for detergents and toiletries are made.

Our own chemical plant. An X-ray image of the abdomen showing the large intestine.

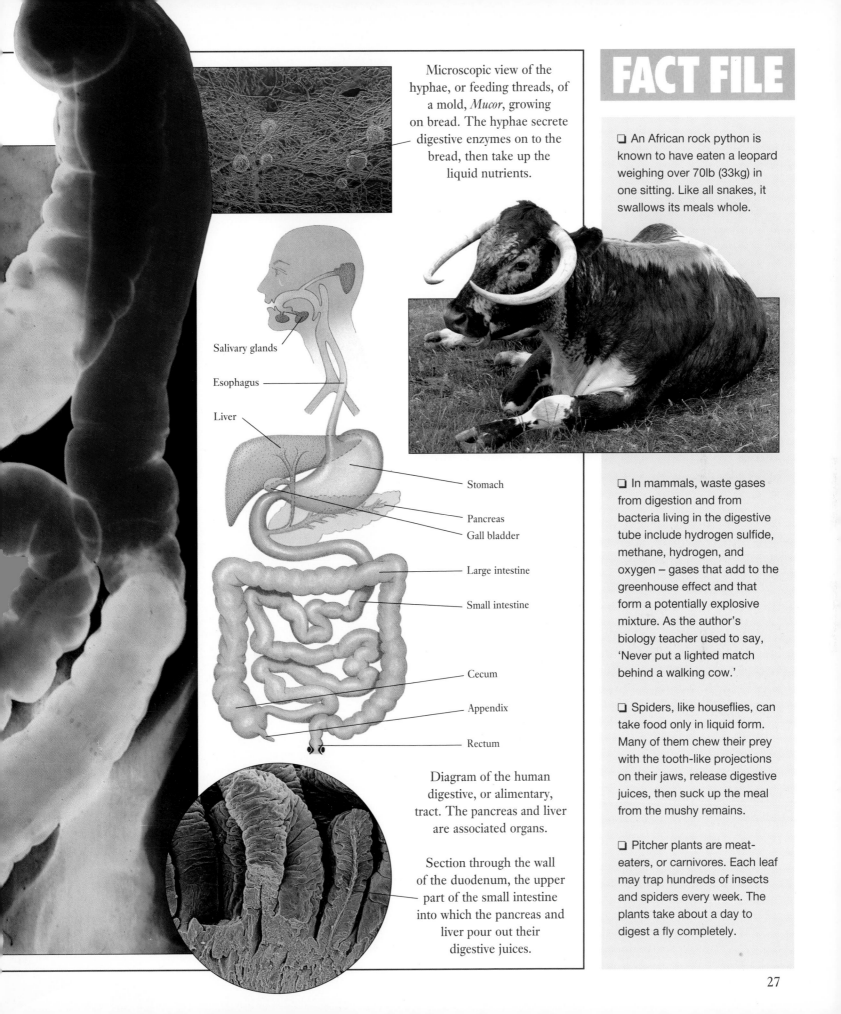

Microscopic view of the hyphae, or feeding threads, of a mold, *Mucor*, growing on bread. The hyphae secrete digestive enzymes on to the bread, then take up the liquid nutrients.

Salivary glands

Esophagus

Liver

Stomach

Pancreas

Gall bladder

Large intestine

Small intestine

Cecum

Appendix

Rectum

Diagram of the human digestive, or alimentary, tract. The pancreas and liver are associated organs.

Section through the wall of the duodenum, the upper part of the small intestine into which the pancreas and liver pour out their digestive juices.

FACT FILE

❑ An African rock python is known to have eaten a leopard weighing over 70lb (33kg) in one sitting. Like all snakes, it swallows its meals whole.

❑ In mammals, waste gases from digestion and from bacteria living in the digestive tube include hydrogen sulfide, methane, hydrogen, and oxygen – gases that add to the greenhouse effect and that form a potentially explosive mixture. As the author's biology teacher used to say, 'Never put a lighted match behind a walking cow.'

❑ Spiders, like houseflies, can take food only in liquid form. Many of them chew their prey with the tooth-like projections on their jaws, release digestive juices, then suck up the meal from the mushy remains.

❑ Pitcher plants are meat-eaters, or carnivores. Each leaf may trap hundreds of insects and spiders every week. The plants take about a day to digest a fly completely.

Energy for life – burning fuel and creating wastes

Violet-stained starch grains – a potato's microscopic power packs to be used for energy to develop buds and shoots.

Food made by plants and taken in by animals is used in three ways: to produce energy, to build new cells for growth, and to renew and replace dead or dying cells. Whatever an organism's diet, however, some of its food material cannot be digested. For example, we cannot digest cellulose, the major constituent of leafy green vegetables such as lettuce and spinach. The undigested part of our meals is got rid of as feces. The major energy source in foods are carbohydrates such as glucose and starch. Inside the body, these are burned in a similar way to the coal that is burned in a steam engine to work a pump. But the process produces neither smoke nor fire. To burn coal, oxygen from the air is needed, but living things can 'burn' food in the absence of oxygen gas, using instead oxygen-containing chemicals such as calcium sulfate and sodium nitrate. Coal comprises mainly carbon, and when it is burned the chemical energy within it is released as heat. Carbon dioxide gas is produced as the main waste product. When living things burn food, much of the chemical energy released is harnessed within special energy-storing molecules in cells. These are nature's units of currency. They are 'spent' within each cell, or are 'exchanged' for building- or repair-molecules with other cells. The by-products are carbon dioxide and water.

Steam billows from the cooling towers of a coal-fired power station. Inside, coal is burned to heat water to make steam that drives turbines.

On a cold morning, mountaineers turn toward the Sun so its heat energy warms them. One of them also drinks a warming cup of hot coffee.

❏ There are billions of bacteria living inside our intestines. They help us digest food and make vitamin K, needed for normal blood clotting. Bacteria in the stomachs of ruminant animals – those that chew the cud, such as cows, deer, camels, and giraffes – break down the cellulose in plant tissues and make the products available to their hosts.

❏ The energy value of food is measured in kilocalories or kilojoules. 1 kilocalorie equals 4.2 kilojoules. The average adult person needs about 3,000 kilocalories a day. This is enough energy to heat up and boil away a gallon (3.7 liters) of ice-cold water.

❏ Feces are a mixture of water (about 65 percent by weight), dietary waste, bacteria, and cells sluffed off the insides of the digestive tube. Nothing they contain has really entered the cells of the body and so, by definition, they are not *excreted* from the body, just eliminated.

The Sun is the powerhouse for life on Earth. Its light provides energy to plant leaves – this is a tobacco leaf seen in section – to make food by photosynthesis.

Exchange of gases

Respiration is one of the characteristics of living things. It is a series of chemical changes that release energy from food materials. Most plants and animals 'burn' their food in processes requiring oxygen gas and producing carbon dioxide and water as wastes. This is called aerobic respiration. Many bacteria and fungi, however, respire in the absence of oxygen. They only partly break down carbohydrates, producing as wastes carbon dioxide and one of a variety of acids and alcohols. Where alcohols are produced, the process is known as fermentation, and we have put this to good use in the making of beers and wines. Whichever form of respiration an organism uses – and some, like ourselves, can use both – it must get rid of the waste products. If they are allowed to build up to high levels, they will eventually poison the organism. Green plants exchange oxygen and carbon dioxide through tiny pores in the underside of their leaves. Small creatures usually exchange these gases across the surface of their bodies. We breathe in air rich in oxygen and breathe out air containing lots of carbon dioxide. So there is a constant natural recycling of gases in the air. For millions of years, the amounts of these two gases in the air has remained constant. But we are now upsetting this balance of nature as we burn fossil fuels – coal, oil, and natural gas.

An albino axolotl, a salamander, with its necklace of feathery gills where exchange of oxygen and carbon dioxide takes place between the water and the axolotl's blood.

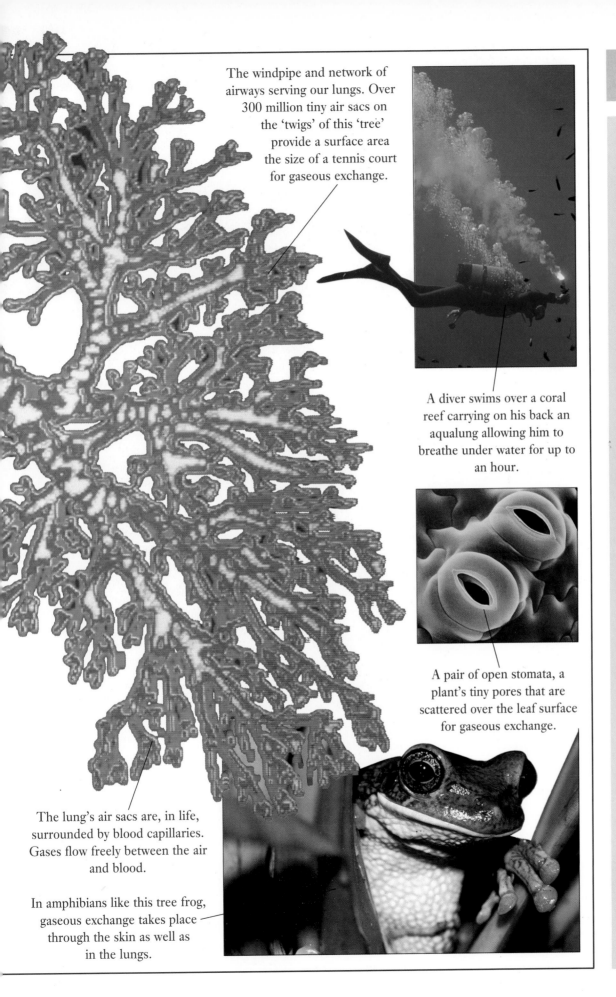

The windpipe and network of airways serving our lungs. Over 300 million tiny air sacs on the 'twigs' of this 'tree' provide a surface area the size of a tennis court for gaseous exchange.

A diver swims over a coral reef carrying on his back an aqualung allowing him to breathe under water for up to an hour.

A pair of open stomata, a plant's tiny pores that are scattered over the leaf surface for gaseous exchange.

The lung's air sacs are, in life, surrounded by blood capillaries. Gases flow freely between the air and blood.

In amphibians like this tree frog, gaseous exchange takes place through the skin as well as in the lungs.

❏ In Brazil, up to 2 million automobiles are powered with the help of bacteria. The cars run on gasohol, a fuel created by mixing a little gasoline with an alcohol made by the fermentation of sugar cane by bacteria.

❏ At rest, the average adult person breathes in and out about 16 times a minute. With each breath, about 30 cubic inches (500ml) of fresh and used air are exchanged. So each minute enough air is exchanged by one person to almost fill two 1-gallon (3.8-l) cans of gasoline. During exercise, this value can increase 25 times.

❏ Nitrogen gas makes up more than 75 percent of the air we breathe in. Of the rest, oxygen is 21 percent and carbon dioxide only 0.03 percent. The air we breathe out contains only 16.5 percent oxygen but 4 percent carbon dioxide. The changes are brought about by respiration.

❏ When life first evolved on Earth more than 3,500 million years ago, there was no oxygen in the air, but lots of carbon dioxide, hydrogen, methane, and ammonia. The oxygen now present is the product of photosynthesis by plants, algae, and bacteria that have lived since that time and that are alive today. Destroy all the forests of the world, and life as we know it will cease to exist.

The circulatory system

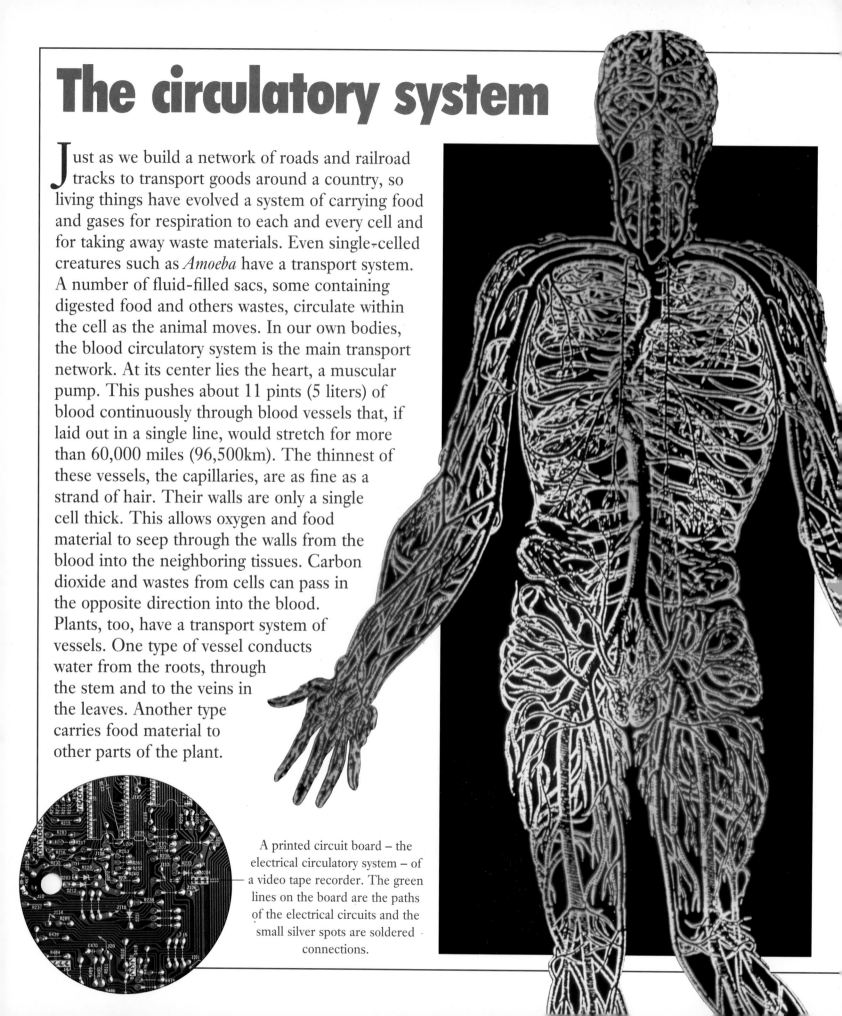

Just as we build a network of roads and railroad tracks to transport goods around a country, so living things have evolved a system of carrying food and gases for respiration to each and every cell and for taking away waste materials. Even single-celled creatures such as *Amoeba* have a transport system. A number of fluid-filled sacs, some containing digested food and others wastes, circulate within the cell as the animal moves. In our own bodies, the blood circulatory system is the main transport network. At its center lies the heart, a muscular pump. This pushes about 11 pints (5 liters) of blood continuously through blood vessels that, if laid out in a single line, would stretch for more than 60,000 miles (96,500km). The thinnest of these vessels, the capillaries, are as fine as a strand of hair. Their walls are only a single cell thick. This allows oxygen and food material to seep through the walls from the blood into the neighboring tissues. Carbon dioxide and wastes from cells can pass in the opposite direction into the blood. Plants, too, have a transport system of vessels. One type of vessel conducts water from the roots, through the stem and to the veins in the leaves. Another type carries food material to other parts of the plant.

A printed circuit board – the electrical circulatory system – of a video tape recorder. The green lines on the board are the paths of the electrical circuits and the small silver spots are soldered connections.

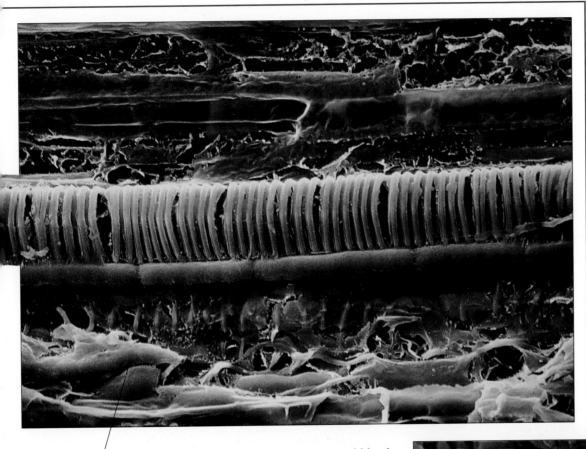

❏ On a hot day, a big tree will lose many tens of gallons of water from its leaves. This causes the leaves literally to suck up water from the roots. The suction pressure is so great that a constant stream of water can be drawn up a tree more than 300ft (91m) tall.

❏ The leaf-like folds of skin on the gills of a fish such as a cod provide a surface area about the same as that of a double-size bed. The folds are filled with blood capillaries so that, as water flows over them, exchange of oxygen and carbon dioxide can take place in a split-second.

The xylem or water-conducting vessels of a pea plant, magnified about ×100 lifesize. The central vessel has spiraled strengthening tissue.

Tiny erythrocytes or red blood cells, like these seen densely packed into a blood capillary, constantly circulate the body, picking up oxygen in the lungs and releasing it in body tissues, where it is used to 'burn' food.

The common earthworm, one of the lowliest of creatures with a blood circulatory system. It has five pairs of heartlike blood pumps.

False-color version of the human venous system as drawn by Renaissance anatomist Andreas Vesalius in 1543. Veins carry blood back to the heart from all parts of the body.

❏ Every drop of your blood contains more than 5 million red cells, 10,000 white cells and 250,000 platelets. The red cells contain hemoglobin, an iron compound to which oxygen readily binds. The white cells combat bacteria and viruses. Blood platelets help blood to clot.

Pumps and valves

The blood-pump of this tiny water flea shows as a red blob in its belly.

How does a water pistol or squirt gun shoot out a jet of water? What stops air rushing out of a bicycle tire? Why doesn't blood rush to your head when you do a handstand? The answers are pumps and valves. A pump is a device for forcing liquids or gases into or out of something.

A valve is a door-like device that opens and closes to control the flow of a liquid or gas through an opening. As you squeeze the trigger of a squirt gun, you apply a pressure to the water inside. This causes an inlet valve to close, an outlet valve to open, and a piston-pump to eject the water. Similarly, once you have pumped air into a tire, a valve stops the air escaping. In your body, valves in the heart ensure blood is pumped in only one direction. Valves in your veins prevent backflow against the force of gravity. Plants, too, have types of pumps and valves. So do electronic toys. In plants, some cells actively take in water from neighboring cells. As they fill, their liquid contents are forced against their walls. This pump-effect gives the cells rigidity and in this way they support the plant. The leaf pores of plants are each enclosed by two cells that together act like a valve to restrict the flow of gases. In an electronic toy, the batteries produce an electric current – a flow of electrons – in the wires. The current flows through electronic devices such as transistors and resistors that allow, prevent, or limit its passage, just like valves.

Illustration of the human heart, about four times lifesize. The yellow fibers are nerves controlling the pumping cycle.

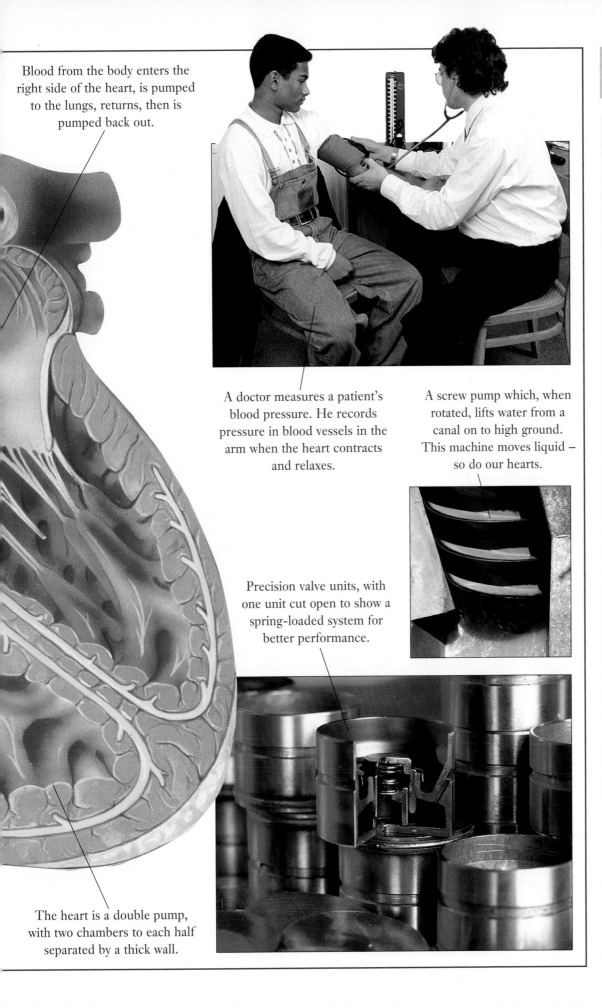

Blood from the body enters the right side of the heart, is pumped to the lungs, returns, then is pumped back out.

A doctor measures a patient's blood pressure. He records pressure in blood vessels in the arm when the heart contracts and relaxes.

A screw pump which, when rotated, lifts water from a canal on to high ground. This machine moves liquid – so do our hearts.

Precision valve units, with one unit cut open to show a spring-loaded system for better performance.

The heart is a double pump, with two chambers to each half separated by a thick wall.

The liver – the body's own factory

The liver is often described as the body's chemical factory. It is the largest organ in the body and carries out at least 500 different chemical reactions. That is more than is needed to process crude oil into gasoline, diesel fuel, bitumen, paraffin waxes, plastics, polishes, adhesives, paints, and detergents. Most of the liver's activities are concerned with producing substances needed for digestion and blood clotting, and for storing food materials. Excess sugar in the body is stored as the chemical glycogen. The average adult has about 4 ounces (110g) of glycogen in the liver. When our muscles need lots of energy quickly – during swimming or a game of tennis, for example – the liver converts glycogen into sugars and releases them into the bloodstream. The liver is also a major source of body heat – a product of all its chemistry – and is a blood purifier. In ancient times the liver was called the seat of life and, after a person died, their liver may have been removed and examined to make predictions about the future. (A palm-reader interpreting the lines on your hands is a modern equivalent.) Every vertebrate (animal with a backbone) has a liver and cannot live without it. Less complex animals, and plants, do not have an equivalent organ.

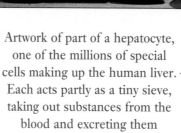

Storing steel cans containing low-level radioactive waste. Some of it is reprocessed as are some biochemicals in the liver.

Artwork of part of a hepatocyte, one of the millions of special cells making up the human liver. Each acts partly as a tiny sieve, taking out substances from the blood and excreting them in the bile.

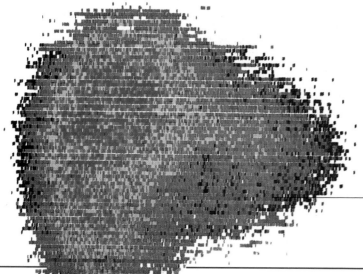

A map (called a scintigram) of build-up of a radioactive chemical introduced into the liver from the bloodstream. An even distribution, as here, indicates a healthy liver.

Each microscopic liver cell is crowded with different organelles, including membranes studded with ribosomes (blue spheres), the sites of protein production, and mitochondria (orange ovals), the cell's powerhouses.

An all-American kid, with her daily intake of food – all to be processed by her liver to produce energy.

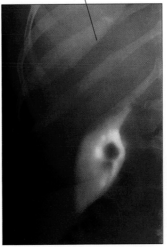

X-ray image of the gall-bladder (orange) showing two gallstones (dark circular areas) formed from excess fats in the diet.

❏ Among the chemicals found in the liver are the metals magnesium, iron, copper, zinc, manganese, and cobalt.

❏ Every day 200,000 million red blood cells die and break up. The hemoglobin they contain – each one carries more than 280 million molecules – is collected by cells in the liver. Then it is passed via the circulatory system to bone marrow, where new red cells are made.

❏ The liver partly acts like a catalytic converter on a modern automobile. The converter modifies polluting exhaust gases from the engine so that they are harmless. The liver modifies alcohol, drugs, and poisons produced by bacteria in the intestines so that they are no longer toxic.

❏ In an adult person, the liver weighs up to 4lb (1.8kg) and, at rest, contains 25 percent of the body's blood.

❏ The human liver produces up to 2 pints (1.1 liter) of bile per day. Bile contains some chemicals which help digestion, and lots of waste products from the breakdown of foodstuffs, hormones, and drugs. It is stored in the gall-bladder then released into the duodenum.

❏ One superstition suggests that the liver of a coward holds no blood – hence the expression, 'lily-livered.'

Getting rid of wastes

Beneath the tongue, crocodiles have special salt-excreting glands to help them maintain a constant blood salt level.

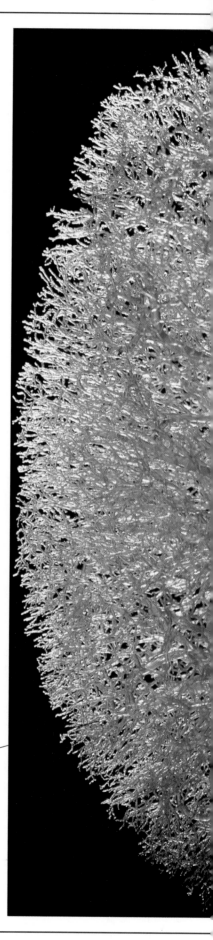

The lactic acid that gives buttermilk, yoghurt, and cheese their flavor, the acetic acid of vinegar, the alcohols of beers and wines, and the citric acid of dyes and inks, are all natural waste products. Probably so too are many of the antibiotics that fungi produce that destroy bacteria. Others include carbon dioxide and water from aerobic respiration (see page 30), and ammonia. The process by which these are removed from the body is called excretion. Many plants store wastes such as salts and acids in their leaves and get rid of them when they shed the leaves. In small animals, the wastes simply pass out through the body surface or are collected in small sacs within the cell. When these are full, they move to the cell surface, burst, release their contents, then reform. Vertebrates excrete through their lungs or gills, the skin, and via the kidneys. The kidneys are composed of tens of thousands of microscopic filter units. They filter out all small materials from the blood – broken-down food substances, water, and wastes – then put back any that are essential. This leaves a liquid, urine, containing unwanted materials, which is passed from the body. Industrial filter units, such as those in air-conditioning systems, sewage works and power station chimneys, work in a different way. Instead of removing many substances from a mix and sorting them into useful and waste materials, they remove just the unwanted materials to leave clean air or water.

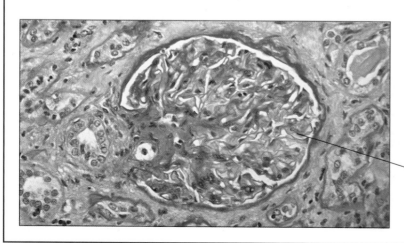

The tiny filtration units in the kidneys are called nephrons. There are hundreds of thousands of these in each kidney.

A glomerulus, one of many thousands of tiny knots of blood capillaries and Bowman's capsules or filter-cups within each human kidney. Around it are kidney tubules seen end-on.

Resin cast of the blood supply to a human kidney. Normally about 25 percent of the heart's output of blood with each beat is shunted through the kidneys for filtration – that is about 2 pints (1 liter) a minute.

Birds such as these nesting Imperial shags produce a paste-like excreta we call guano.

A car catalytic converter, which reduces the toxic gases from a petrol or diesel engine by converting exhaust fumes into harmless products.

❏ The human kidneys are each about the size of the palm of a hand and weigh 5oz (140g). They contain over a million filter units and each day produce 2 to 3 pints (about 1.3 liters) of urine.

❏ Guano, the semi-solid excrement of birds and bats, is used in parts of South America and Southeast Asia as a fertilizer. It is rich in nitrates and phosphates needed by plants.

❏ The West-Southwest Water Treatment Plant in Chicago, U.S.A., is the world's largest sewage works. Its filters treat 835 million gallons (3,160 million liters) of liquid waste from the kitchens and bathrooms of the homes of nearly 3 million people.

❏ Spinach and rhubarb plants store crystals of unwanted oxalic acid in their leaves. The acid is poisonous and corrosive. The leaves are safe to eat only after they are cooked – during which a metal saucepan becomes etched clean by the acid!

Keeping at the right temperature

A Marine iguana basks in the sun on a rock in the Galapagos Islands. Like all reptiles, sunbathing is its way of raising its body temperature.

Whales, such as this Humpback, have a thick layer of fat, known as blubber, under the skin which keeps them warm when they are in icy waters.

Acoal-burning boiler heats water. The boiler pump pushes the hot water through pipes and radiators, where warmth from the water escapes into the air. A thermostat monitors room temperature and switches the boiler on or off to keep a constant level of warmth in the room. This is the basis of a typical home central heating system. But in many ways it also describes our body's temperature-regulating system. Our muscles and liver are the boilers, our blood the hot water, the heart is the water pump, and the blood vessels are the pipes and radiators. The body's thermostat, the hypothalamus, lies within the brain. It maintains our internal temperature at around 98.5°F (37°C). Below about 85°F (29°C) and we become sleepy and semi-conscious. Above 105°F (41°C), we experience convulsions, delerium, and go into a coma. The need for a constant body temperature is primarily because enzymes, the catalysts vital to body chemistry, function best around 100°F (37.8°C). When we get too hot – through exercise or illness – the hypothalamus causes more blood to reach the surface of the skin and heat to escape from the body. It also promotes sweating – which gives a cooling effect – and encourages us to take off our clothes or switch on the air-conditioning, take in cold foods and drinks, and to rest. As body temperature falls, the hypothalamus initiates the opposite effect, including making us shiver, which produces heat. Biologists popularly refer to birds and mammals as warm-blooded, and to animals such as fish, frogs, and snakes as cold-blooded. We keep our bodies warm by burning food, whereas a cold-blooded creature has to rely on its surroundings to keep its body temperature constant. A crocodile, for instance, basks in the sun to warm up and slinks into water to cool down. Yet many cold-blooded animals maintain a body temperature many degrees higher than our own. In winter, some cold-blooded creatures, particularly certain reptiles, will hibernate in order to slow their metabolisms during the cold spell.

Microscopic view of one of the millions of sweat pores in human skin. Sweat evaporates using excess body heat, and so cools the blood.

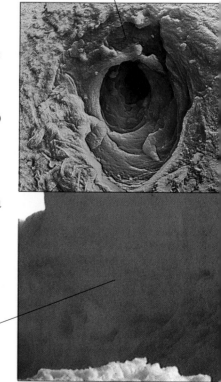

In a den that she hollows out deep in the snow, a Polar bear will give birth to her cubs and keep them there until their fur and blubber are thick enough to insulate them from the cold.

A lioness pants, losing heat as the water vapor in her breath evaporates. For birds, panting is the only way of cooling the body; they lack sweat glands.

With their thick, oily fur and blubber, Polar bears can withstand arctic temperatures of −40°F (−40°C).

Levers and joints

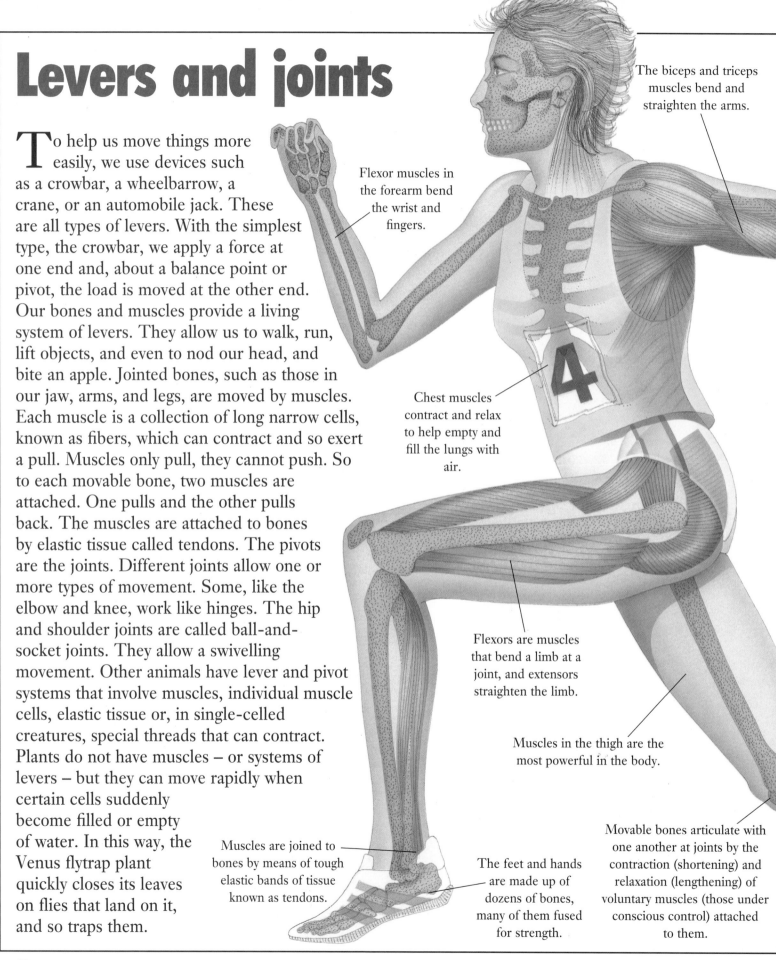

To help us move things more easily, we use devices such as a crowbar, a wheelbarrow, a crane, or an automobile jack. These are all types of levers. With the simplest type, the crowbar, we apply a force at one end and, about a balance point or pivot, the load is moved at the other end. Our bones and muscles provide a living system of levers. They allow us to walk, run, lift objects, and even to nod our head, and bite an apple. Jointed bones, such as those in our jaw, arms, and legs, are moved by muscles. Each muscle is a collection of long narrow cells, known as fibers, which can contract and so exert a pull. Muscles only pull, they cannot push. So to each movable bone, two muscles are attached. One pulls and the other pulls back. The muscles are attached to bones by elastic tissue called tendons. The pivots are the joints. Different joints allow one or more types of movement. Some, like the elbow and knee, work like hinges. The hip and shoulder joints are called ball-and-socket joints. They allow a swivelling movement. Other animals have lever and pivot systems that involve muscles, individual muscle cells, elastic tissue or, in single-celled creatures, special threads that can contract. Plants do not have muscles – or systems of levers – but they can move rapidly when certain cells suddenly become filled or empty of water. In this way, the Venus flytrap plant quickly closes its leaves on flies that land on it, and so traps them.

The biceps and triceps muscles bend and straighten the arms.

Flexor muscles in the forearm bend the wrist and fingers.

Chest muscles contract and relax to help empty and fill the lungs with air.

Flexors are muscles that bend a limb at a joint, and extensors straighten the limb.

Muscles in the thigh are the most powerful in the body.

Muscles are joined to bones by means of tough elastic bands of tissue known as tendons.

The feet and hands are made up of dozens of bones, many of them fused for strength.

Movable bones articulate with one another at joints by the contraction (shortening) and relaxation (lengthening) of voluntary muscles (those under conscious control) attached to them.

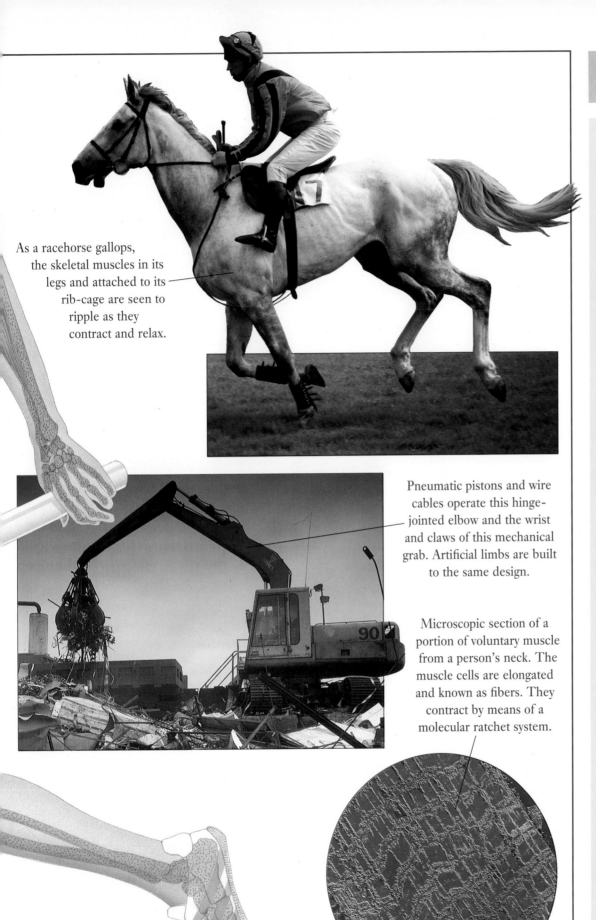

As a racehorse gallops, the skeletal muscles in its legs and attached to its rib-cage are seen to ripple as they contract and relax.

Pneumatic pistons and wire cables operate this hinge-jointed elbow and the wrist and claws of this mechanical grab. Artificial limbs are built to the same design.

Microscopic section of a portion of voluntary muscle from a person's neck. The muscle cells are elongated and known as fibers. They contract by means of a molecular ratchet system.

❏ To jump, a flea uses not muscles but the release of energy from a compressed material, resilin, in its hind legs. This works rather like a rubber shock-absorber on an automobile. As the car goes over a bump, the rubber is compressed. Then it releases energy, pushing the vehicle up to keep it level on the road and provide a smooth side.

❏ Compared to us, frogs and toads have especially long hind legs with powerful muscles. 'Santjie,' the world record holder for the longest jump by an amphibian, in a competition involving three consecutive leaps, covered 33½ ft (10.3m). The human triple jump record is around 60ft (18m), while the long jump record currently stands at 29ft 4⅓in (8.95m).

❏ The most powerful cranes in the world are aboard an Italian salvage seacraft, *Micoperi 7000*. They can each lift loads weighing 7,716 tons (7,000 tonnes).

❏ Single-celled creatures such as *Paramecium* and *Euglena*, numerous bacteria, and the sperm cells of animals, mosses, and seaweeds, move by beating tiny hair- or whip-like structures on their surfaces, known as cilia and flagella.

Walking and running

Animals move, plants do not. This is often cited as the main difference between the two. Indeed, most plants do not move about as complete organisms – some microscopic plants do – yet not all animals are fully mobile. Adult barnacles, for example, spend all their lives firmly attached to a rock, a ship's hull, or the wooden pillar of a jetty. Those animals that are mobile are adapted for movement on land, in the sea, in the air, or various combinations of these. We are all-rounders. We can walk and run, climb and jump, swim fairly well, and, by pedalling human-powered craft, we can even fly. Land mammals get about on legs, while other terrestrial animals, such as snakes and earthworms, haul their bodies over the ground. Movement from place to place is known as locomotion, and animals do this to find food or shelter, to escape predators, or to search for a mate for sexual reproduction. Walking is slow locomotion, running is fast. But mechanically they are quite different. In walking, there are stages when parts of both feet are on the ground at the same time. We lift one foot, just as we set down the other foot. In contrast, running involves stages when both feet are off the ground simultaneously. Whichever way we get about, our muscles and skeleton provide the necessary power, and food is the fuel.

A humanoid robot, built with arm and leg joints that mimic the mechanics of our own skeletal joints.

A horse walks taking four distinct steps, for example in the sequence offside hind, offside fore, nearside hind, nearside fore.

Sprinters shoot from their running blocks at the start of a race. They are converting their stored energy into kinetic energy.

A scan of a person's knees, revealing the joint cartilages in red and white. A lubricant, the synovial fluid, ensures the joint moves freely.

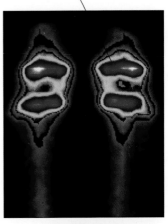

The sprinter's muscles provide driving force, his pounding lungs and heart the vital oxygen and blood his muscle cells need.

Apollo 11 astronaut Edwin 'Buzz' Aldrin, the second person to walk on the Moon, took more than one giant step for mankind. His footprints will stay on the Moon unchanged as there are no winds or rain to erase them.

FACT FILE

Crawling and climbing

The British Scorpion armored fighting vehicle is the fastest in the world. It can reach speeds of over 50mph (80km/h). It moves on flexible 'caterpillar' tracks wrapped around the vehicle's wheels. These spread the weight of the tank so that it does not sink into soft ground as it crawls forward. Many types of animal can also crawl, but using muscle-power not engines, and at only a fraction of the Scorpion's speed. They do so by means of rhythmic waves of muscle contraction and relaxation that pass along the body. In a crawling earthworm, for example, segments in some parts of its body become short and fat and others long and thin. Snails crawl on a muscular foot covered with slimy mucus. A snake crawls by 'swimming' or 'gliding' over the ground, with bends of the body starting at the head and traveling to the tail. It pushes the scales on its skin against rough ground, stones, and plants for leverage. Plant roots can 'crawl' over the surface of the soil as they grow using tiny hairs on their surfaces to absorb nutrients and gain a grip. Climbers of the natural world include ants, caterpillars, crabs, lizards, frogs, monkeys, ivy, and pea and bean plants. Among animals, adaptations for climbing include suction pads on feet or fins (houseflies and mudskippers), claws for digging into uprights such as tree trunks (cats, woodpeckers, and beetles), and grasping hands (monkeys and apes). Plants have evolved stems that wrap around upright supports (honeysuckle, strangler figs, and lianas), leaves modified as clinging tendrils (sweet pea and clematis), suckers and special aerial roots that act as anchors (ivy). We can crawl and climb using our arms and legs, hands and feet in coordinated action.

By the age of about 8 months most children can crawl, although some, like the author's two boys, never crawled and instead bottom-shuffled. Climbing is a skill acquired by about 2 years of age.

A Swallowtail butterfly caterpillar crawls along a stem. Its three pairs of jointed true legs at the front bear claws. Its four pairs of unjointed fleshy prolegs have rows of tiny hooks at the ends.

Young climbers 'learning the ropes,' including abseiling, the skill of descending by almost walking down the rockface.

The space shuttle *Columbia* is moved from the Vehicle Assembly Building to the launch pad on a giant caterpillar-track vehicle that crawls along a roadway at less than 1mph (1.6km/h)

This Gray rat snake will climb stealthily in trees to prey on birds or to take their eggs from nests to eat.

❑ Geckos are small lizards that can hang upside-down from ceilings and scamper up a glass windowpane, perhaps in pursuit of a fly to eat. They can do this by means of many ridges on the underside of their feet that grip on to any tiny ridges and bumps on surfaces.

❑ The 'ropes' used by fictional adventurers like Tarzan and Indiana Jones to swing through jungles are the living stems of climbing plants called lianas. These stems can reach 1,000ft (300m) in length.

❑ Between February and May 1990, mountaineer Timothy Macartney-Snape climbed from sea level to the highest point in the world, the top of Mt Everest (29,078ft/8,863m). He was the first, and so far the only, person to have done this.

❑ Adult eels can crawl over ground almost as well as a snake. They do so to migrate from rivers and ponds into the sea where they mate and lay their eggs. Juvenile eels swim from the sea into fresh-water areas, where they reach maturity.

❑ Snakes do not crawl by 'walking on their ribs' as was once believed, but by pushing back against the ground with the enlarged scales on the underside of their skin. 'Sidewinding' is a form of snake movement that is a mixture of crawling and almost leaping.

Swimming and diving

The fastest swimmer in the seas is the Bluefin tuna. It can reach 65mph (104km/h). Its long, slender, smooth body, with fins top, bottom, and sides, is typical of fish adapted to move through the water with ease. We have adopted this body plan in the design of all sorts of sea craft, from submarines and torpedoes to racing yachts and hydrofoils. While we can use oars, paddles, and propellers to drive craft forward in water, most fish use flexing movements of their bodies like a crawling snake. The fins provide stability and a means of steering. However, whales, porpoises, turtles, seals, penguins, water beetles, and many single-celled creatures, do have paddle-like structures – tail, flippers, wings, cilia – with which they push against the water to propel themselves forward. Cuttlefish and squid swim slowly by waving their arms about, but use jet propulsion to move quickly. They take in water at the front of their bodies, then squirt it out forcefully to produce thrust. (In a similar way, a jet engine takes in air, uses it to burn fuel, then forces out the expanding gases to create forward movement.) Diving requires the ability not only to swim well, but also to breathe underwater and to cope with changes in temperature and pressure in the environment. The deeper one dives, the colder the water and the greater the pressure on the body. Animals such as fish can obtain oxygen from water, but turtles, birds, and sea mammals – seals, whales, dugongs, and so on – must surface regularly to take a fresh breath of air. In general, an animal's body is heavier than water, making it sink. To float or to keep at a certain depth in the water, most marine creatures have gas-filled floats, which in fish are known as swimbladders. Oxygen and other gases are released into the sacs from the bloodstream as required. Submarines use a comparable system to dive and surface, taking in and expelling water from buoyancy tanks.

Bottlenose dolphins break through the surface of the water as they reach speeds of 25mph (40km/h).

Bony fish, like these colorful Butterfly fish that live on coral reefs, have swimbladders for buoyancy and several pairs of fins for propulsion through the water.

❏ Sperm whales can dive to depths of more than 7,000ft (2,120m) and stay underwater for about 90 minutes before having to surface for fresh air.

❏ In 1960, *Trieste II*, a research submarine, descended 36,300ft (11,000m) into the Pacific Ocean – the deepest dive on record. Modern nuclear submarines can stay underwater for up to 3 years, but most dive for only about a week or two at a time.

❏ Even with an air-supply, human beings cannot dive to more than about 400ft (120m) as beyond this depth water pressure on the body gets too great for the human body to endure. We can swim at speeds of up to 5½mph (8.8km/h).

❏ The coconut palm, characteristic of holidaymakers' 'paradise' islands, produces seeds with a woolly husk that keeps them afloat in the sea for weeks. The palm originated in Southeast Asia but 'swam' thousands of miles with the currents to colonize all the warm parts of the world.

As this diver nears the water, he will straighten his body to 'cut' through the surface with the minimum of splash.

Synchronized swimming, the latest Olympic water sport. The aquatic acrobats move in unison on and below the surface of the water in time to music.

Outer defenses

A male Hercules beetle of Central America, its tough outer casing extends as a horn up to 2½in (6.25cm) long.

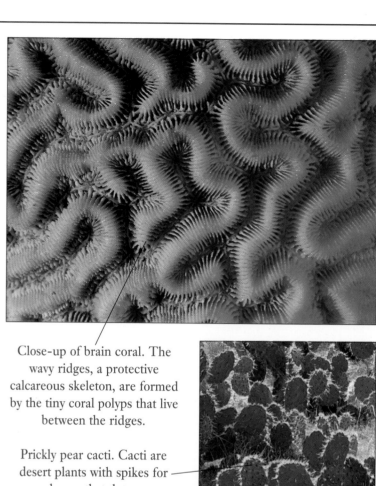

Close-up of brain coral. The wavy ridges, a protective calcareous skeleton, are formed by the tiny coral polyps that live between the ridges.

Our skin provides protection. It acts as a buffer to bumps and bashes that can damage internal organs. It prevents microbes from entering the body, and shields our insides from the Sun's potentially harmful ultraviolet rays. Compared to many animals, though, we have very thin, soft skin. An elephant and rhinoceros have thick, knobbly skins creating a plate of armor. Dinosaurs probably had a skin like this too. Reptiles and fish have skin bearing tough scales, creating a chain-mail type of protective covering. The skin of arthropods (insects, spiders, crabs, scorpions, millipedes) provides even greater protection. It consists of a casing made from a special protein known as chitin. This offers not only protection, but also support and something for muscles to pull on and so enable movement. Biologists refer to this outer covering as an exoskeleton. It is comparable to the all-over suit of armor used for tanks, particularly as it also provides some defense against predators. In addition to skin, many animals have weapons for defense – stinging cells, spines, horns, and tusks. Plants, too, have outer defenses. Their cells are surrounded by a cellulose wall, which may be impregnated with chemicals for added strength. The bark of trees, consisting of layers of dead cells, is like the tough skin of a rhino. Plant seeds and spores are invariably covered in a tough weatherproof layer of cells, providing protection for long periods. Plant weapons include thorns and spikes, such as those on rosebush stems and cacti.

Prickly pear cacti. Cacti are desert plants with spikes for leaves that deter plant-eating animals.

A Black rhino displaying its pair of horns, and thick, protective skin covering.

A complete human skull, about lifesize. The cranium or braincase is composed of many bones that fuse together in infancy to form a protective box around the delicate brain.

❏ A fully armed knight of the medieval period was virtually encased in plate armor. A typical suit comprised more than 100 steel plates. But like the exoskeleton of arthropods, it had joints and hinges to allow a great deal of movement.

❏ Snakes, scorpions, spiders, and bees will bite or sting and inject poisons in order to defend themselves. A single bee sting can kill an adult person, although some people have survived over 100 such stings at a time.

❏ A dinosaur, *Therizinosaurus cheloniformis*, had the longest claws of any known animal. They were 36in (91cm) long and were probably used for tearing apart other large dinosaurs to eat.

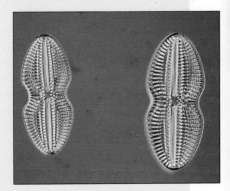

❏ Diatoms look like elaborate pill-boxes, with a lid and a case bearing beautiful patterns of pits or projections. They are in fact single-celled marine algae less than 1/25th of an inch (1mm) across. The silica case prevents the cell collapsing under pressure from the water above.

Inner defenses

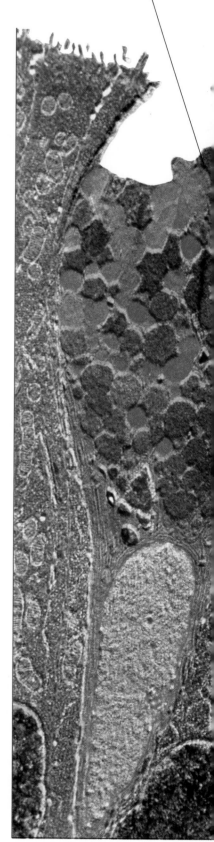

A mucus-secreting goblet cell magnified about ×2,500. Mucus is secreted in the body by cells lining the nasal chambers and the breathing tubes to trap germs and dust particles entering the lungs.

Living things are constantly under attack – from disease-causing bacteria, viruses, and fungi, from parasites, from predators, and from the threat of injury and damage to tissues. While their outer defenses are mainly physical, their inner ones are mostly chemical and cellular. Our own chemical arsenal includes saliva, stomach acid, and the digestive enzymes of the intestines. These destroy most invading microbes. Our cellular defenders include an army of white blood cells. Some of these, known as phagocytes, engulf and digest 'foreign' material. They are like a batallion of hungry *Amoeba* cells within our body. Other white cells, called lymphocytes, produce special chemicals referred to as antibodies. Some of these stick to the outer surface of microbes and make it easier for phagocytes to ingest them. Others neutralize the poisonous chemicals – toxins – secreted by microbes. Together, these white cells comprise the body's immune system. They burst into action when any germ enters the bloodstream. Plants rely almost exclusively on chemical defenses. These include poisons such as cyanide and strychnine, and tannins, which make plant tissues taste unpleasant or indigestible so that a predator leaves them alone. In response to local injury or infection, many plants also produce gums that block their conducting tissues and so limit the area of damage or disease. Most living things have the ability to repair damage that has occurred to them. Repair usually involves a period of new cell growth to replace tissues that have died. This is how our bones mend after a break or fracture. Nervous tissue, however, does not have this ability. Damage to the spinal cord or the brain is invariably serious and permanent.

Our skeleton supports the body, protects internal organs – the ribcage around the lungs, for example – and makes white blood cells which fight germs.

Circular granules near the top of the cell contain the protein mucigen, which combines with water to form mucus.

Scaffolding around the internal strengthening and supporting struts of the Palm House, Kew Gardens, London.

Trapped among strands of the blood-clotting protein, fibrinogen, are a single erythrocyte (center) and several macrophages – white blood cells that engulf and digest invading bacteria and germs.

Hooks and suckers on the head of a tapeworm that lives as a parasite inside wading birds. The worm embeds these organs in the wall of the birds' intestines.

❏ Digitalis – a chemical produced naturally by plants such as foxgloves to deter plant-eating animals – is both deadly and live-saving to us. Eating a few foxglove leaves will cause a massive heart atttack, but small doses of digitalis slow the heart-beat rate and allow an overworked heart to function more efficiently. Doctors prescribe it for various heart disorders.

❏ One of the best hopes for combatting the deadly AIDS virus is to produce a vaccine – a modified form of the virus that, when injected into the body, will stimulate the immune system specifically against the actual disease.

❏ The hydrochloric acid present in our stomach – essential for the action of various digestive enzymes – is strong enough to eat its way instantly through the paper of this book or through a cotton shirt, if it were spilled on these substances.

❏ Some grasshoppers are winning the biological war against the milkweeds plants on which they feed. The insects have evolved an immunity to the milkweeds' natural poisons and in fact store the chemicals in their bodies for use as toxic sprays against birds and reptiles that try and eat them.

Coordination and control

Some of the most powerful computers in the world are onboard the Space Shuttles. Each has a multimillion-word memory and can perform more than 1,000 million calculations a second. Each comprises tens of millions of interconnecting electronic components. The computer is used to guide the spacecraft through space, analyze data from sensors, store them or act upon them, and process information received from mission control on the ground. Our nervous systems are like the Shuttles' computers. They have as many electrical components, can handle as much information with equal speed, and allow us to perform tasks ranging from swimming and playing chess, to memorizing our multiplication tables and reading this book. They also control the actions of our heart, lungs, kidneys, and so on. In fact, no multicellular animal can survive without a nervous system. It provides essential body coordination and control. However, there are other control systems within creatures. Each depends on a high degree of cell-to-cell communication. Different types of cells – muscle and bone, or root and stem – have molecules on their surface that fit together to varying degrees, allowing them more or less to recognize one another and act accordingly. Adjoining cells have actual bridges or systems of canals and lockgates within their membranes, allowing passage of chemicals between their respective cytoplasms. There are also various chemical messengers that influence the activity of certain cells, tissues, and organs. The electrical signals of nervous systems are fast-moving and specific in their effects, whereas chemical messengers work more slowly and bring about general changes. We shall look at these two main systems of communication and control in turn on the pages that follow.

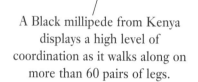

A Black millipede from Kenya displays a high level of coordination as it walks along on more than 60 pairs of legs.

Coordination of vision, balance, and body movement are needed to pole vault over the high bar. This is a high-speed photograph freezing the vaulter in split-second stages of action.

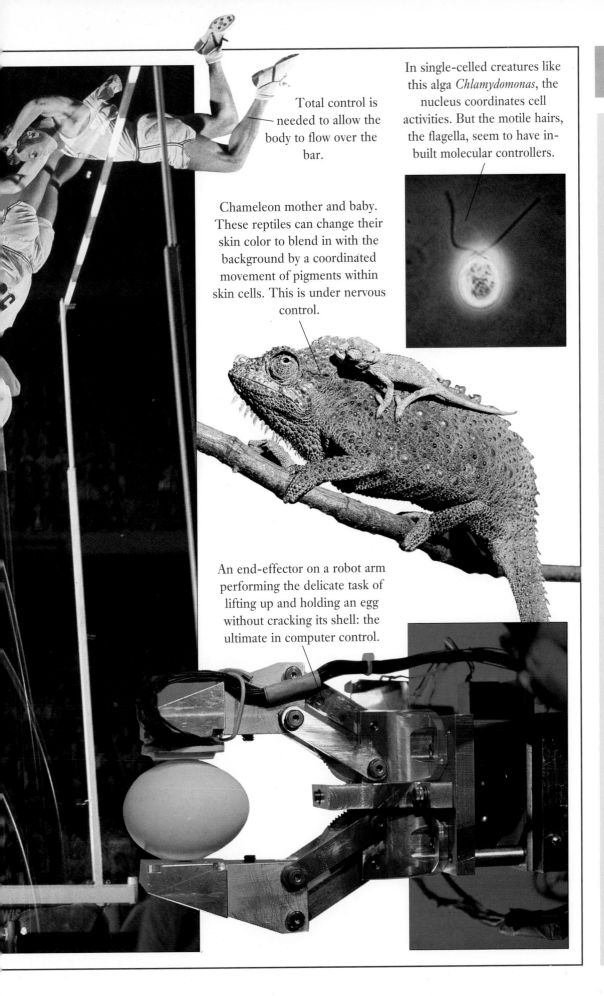

Total control is needed to allow the body to flow over the bar.

In single-celled creatures like this alga *Chlamydomonas*, the nucleus coordinates cell activities. But the motile hairs, the flagella, seem to have in-built molecular controllers.

Chameleon mother and baby. These reptiles can change their skin color to blend in with the background by a coordinated movement of pigments within skin cells. This is under nervous control.

An end-effector on a robot arm performing the delicate task of lifting up and holding an egg without cracking its shell: the ultimate in computer control.

Chemical messengers

Litmus paper used in chemistry to test for acids and alkalis contains a dye extracted from certain lichens that changes color with different conditions. The dye turns red in the presence of acids, blue in alkalis. A similar 'indicator' is contained in breathalyzer units used by police to determine a driver's alcohol intake. Too much alcohol and the indicator turns green. Indicators are chemical messengers. Similar messengers are used by animals such as cats, dogs, and ants, to communicate with others. Cats and dogs urinate on trees and posts to signal to others the limits of their territory. Ants lay odor trails that indicate to one another the direction to and from sources of food. Many living things have internal chemical messengers. These are concerned with the control and coordination of processes such as growth. In mammals, various hormones control the development of reproductive organs and direct the course of pregnancy and birth. Each hormone is secreted into the bloodstream from one organ and brings about changes in another. Hormone-secreting organs are known as glands and in our bodies these include the pituitary and hypothalamus of the brain, the pancreas, the adrenals, and the stomach. In plants, chemical messengers known as auxins control the rate of growth of roots, stems, leaves, and flowers. Others control leaf-fall, the opening of buds, and germination of seeds. Many of these messenger systems involve a feedback system comparable to that used in a car with a cruise control to maintain a constant speed. In the car, a sensor measures the car's speed and boosts fuel flow if speed begins to drop and reduces the flow if the car starts to speed up. In our own bodies, sensors measure the levels of hormones in the blood and direct the secreting organs to raise or lower output to keep conditions constant.

Metamorphosis, the change in body form from larva to adult characteristic of insects and amphibians, is under hormonal control. Here, a Monarch butterfly caterpillar is pupating.

In humans, release of the hormones progesterone and testosterone from the ovaries and testes prepares the body for reproduction.

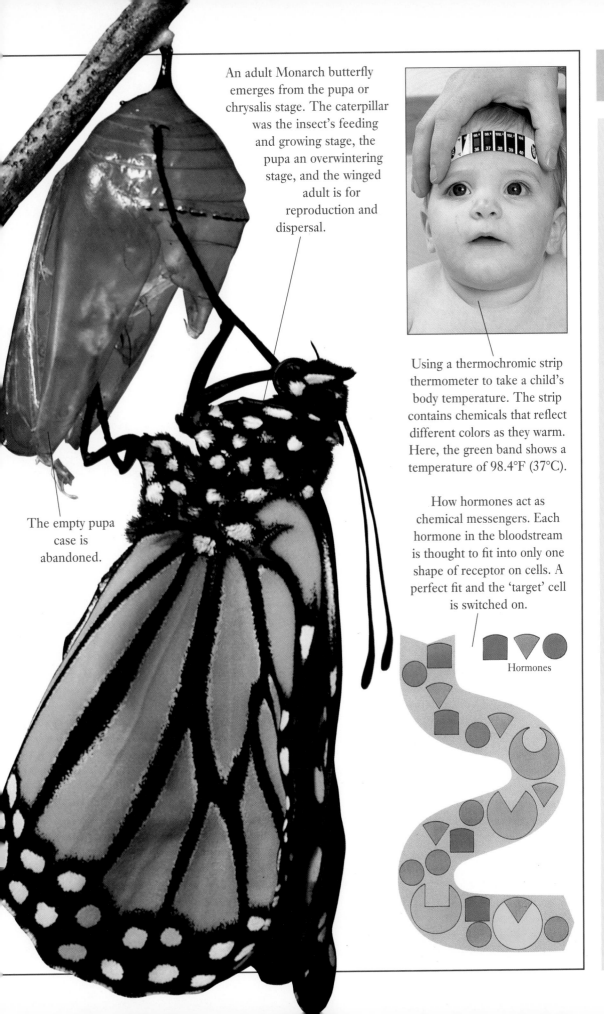

An adult Monarch butterfly emerges from the pupa or chrysalis stage. The caterpillar was the insect's feeding and growing stage, the pupa an overwintering stage, and the winged adult is for reproduction and dispersal.

The empty pupa case is abandoned.

Using a thermochromic strip thermometer to take a child's body temperature. The strip contains chemicals that reflect different colors as they warm. Here, the green band shows a temperature of 98.4°F (37°C).

How hormones act as chemical messengers. Each hormone in the bloodstream is thought to fit into only one shape of receptor on cells. A perfect fit and the 'target' cell is switched on.

Hormones

❑ A chemical messenger known as a pheromone released by a female Atlas moth to advertise that she is ready to mate can be detected by a male moth more than 4 miles (7km) away. He picks up her scent in the air with his huge antennae.

❑ Ethylene, a flammable gas made artificially from petroleum, occurs naturally in plants as a hormone. Once flowers are pollinated, the hormone is released from stem cells and its level in the plant builds up as summer fades, hastening the ripening of the fruit.

❑ Adult salmon ready to mate find their way up to 3,000 miles (4,800km) across open seas back to the very stream in which they were born by recognizing the unique chemical 'signature' of the stream water. Each fish literally smells or tastes its way back home across the vast expanse of ocean.

❑ Certain parasitic worms and fungi that infect ants produce chemical messengers which alter the ants' behavior to the parasites' advantage. Under the influence of these 'drugs,' the ants climb to the top of plants rather than stay on the ground. From this vantage point, the worm larvae and fungal spores are more easily dispersed by the wind. So unwittingly, the ants help to spread the parasites to other ants.

Nerve cells and neural networks

Starfish have a nerve ring within the central disk of the body. The tube-feet can work independently from its impulses.

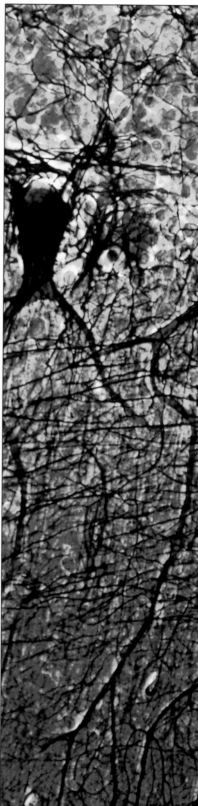

The nervous systems of animals are made up of nerve cells or neurons. There are three main types of neuron – sensory, motor, and connector. Sensory neurons detect changes in the surroundings – technically known as stimuli – and input messages into the system. Motor neurons output messages to muscles, glands, or specialized cells, which produce bodily changes in response to the stimuli. Connector neurons act as go-betweens. Together neurons make up an internal communication network. In lowly creatures, such as jellyfish and *Hydra*, the network comprises a seemingly random collection of neurons spread throughout the body. Each nerve cell makes contact with perhaps half a dozen others. This arrangement is called a nerve net. More advanced animals have evolved a highly structured 'central' nervous system. Here, neurons, or parts of them, are concentrated in discrete units and each neuron makes contact with tens or hundreds of others. Long cablelike structures – nerves – act as high-speed communications links, and there are several swollen areas, known as ganglia, which act as data processing and information exchange units. In vertebrates, one of these ganglia is the brain (see pages 62-63). There are parallels between the nervous system of vertebrates and the components of a computer system. For example, our sense organs – our eyes, ears, nose, tongue, and skin – input information in the same way that a computer keyboard or mouse does. The central processing unit and memory store of a computer is its 'brain.'

Cuttlefish, octopuses, and squid, like this European species, have the most highly developed brains and sense organs among invertebrates.

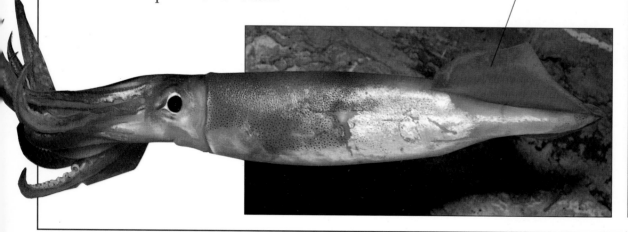

Part of the neural network of the human cerebellum. The four dark cells visible are representative of the largest neurons in the body. Their dendrites extend throughout the cerebellum, which receives input from sense organs and skeletal muscles.

Cell body

Dendrites

Nucleus

Axon

Insulating sheath

Nerve-muscle connection

Muscle fibers

Diagram of a typical nerve cell. Impulses travel from the cell body, along the axon, and to the next neuron or to muscle fibers.

Gridiron pattern of microscopic electrical connections on a wafer of silicon in an integrated circuit from a computer.

❏ In the human nervous system, sensory and motor neurons make up less than 1 percent of all nerve cells. The majority of connector neurons are located in the brain and are concerned with data processing, memory, and interpretation.

❏ Our brains are dying from the day we are born. Every day hundreds of our neurons die and they are never replaced. This probably explains why our mental efficiency decreases with age.

❏ A working robot vision system, Wisard, developed at Brunel University, England, in the 1980s, is based on an electronic model of the neural network inside our brains. It can learn – rather than just be taught (as conventional robots are) – to recognize people's faces.

❏ An insect's 'brain' contains about 10,000 nerve cells – many thousands of times less than the brains of mammals such as ourselves.

Nerve impulses

As you read these words, a constant stream of light rays strikes the sensory neurons at the back of your eyes. The neurons are triggered to fire messages to your brain, where they are interpreted. Messages traveling through the nervous system are known as impulses. They take the form primarily of electrical signals, but chemical messengers are also involved. A nerve impulse rushes along the length of a neuron as a wave of electrical disturbance brought about by molecular changes in the cell membrane. At the tip of the neuron, this prompts the release of chemicals known as neurotransmitters. These flow across the junction, or synaptic gap, with the next neuron, where they create an identical electrical disturbance. In this way, impulses travel from neuron to neuron. They do so at speeds of up to 400ft (120m) a second. As soon as an impulse passes along a neuron, the cell membrane is restored to its normal state. While this is going on, the neuron cannot be triggered. The recovery time, though, is only a few millionths of a second. This action-rest or on-off process, and the fact that impulses can only move one-way across junctions, means that nervous systems work like digital computers. All impulses are electrically the same, and neurons work on an all-or-nothing basis – identical to the 0's and 1's of the binary code. Different stimuli create only different quantities of impulses and these move at various speeds and along certain pathways depending on where they are to take effect.

The leaf of a sundew, a carnivorous plant, covered with sticky-tipped tentacles. Nerve impulse-like changes in the tentacles cause them to curl inward, gripping prey.

A laser light pen is scanned across a bar code, sending on-off electrical messages to a computer for interpretation.

The sundew's tentacles secrete enzymes that digest an insect 'meal.'

An oscilloscope, an instrument that provides a visual image of electrical signals in the form of a graph, is being used to check computer electronics.

Electrodes attached to this boy's head and face record the electrical activity from different parts of his brain in response to stimuli.

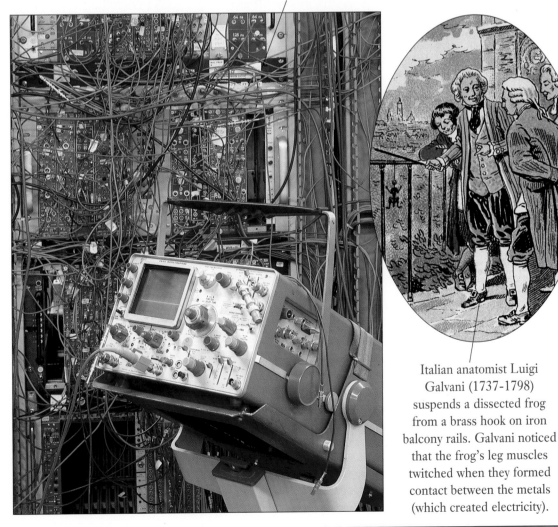

Italian anatomist Luigi Galvani (1737-1798) suspends a dissected frog from a brass hook on iron balcony rails. Galvani noticed that the frog's leg muscles twitched when they formed contact between the metals (which created electricity).

Brain and control centers

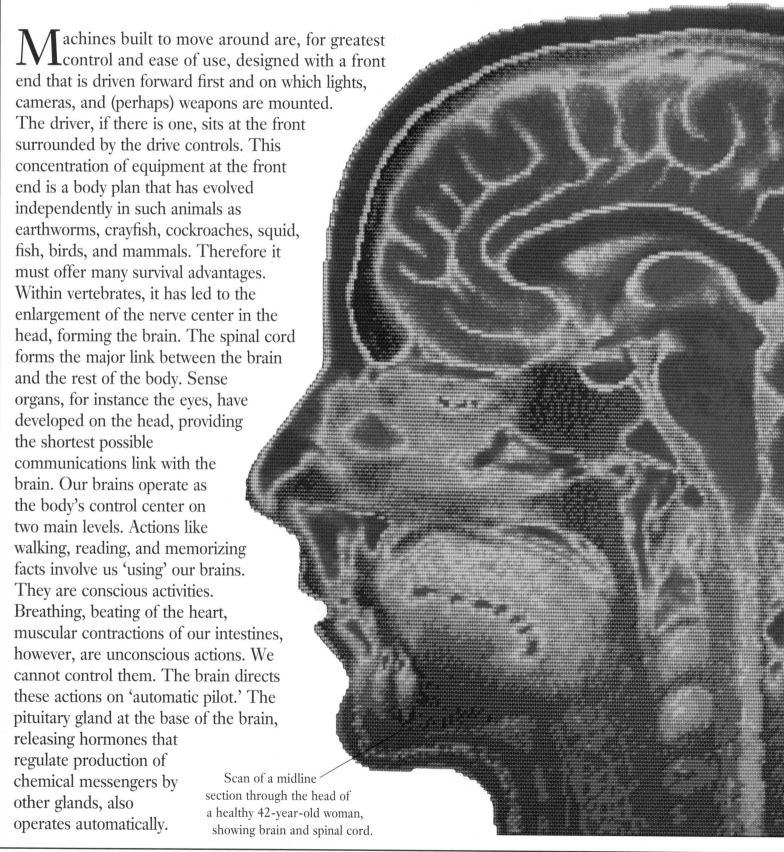

Machines built to move around are, for greatest control and ease of use, designed with a front end that is driven forward first and on which lights, cameras, and (perhaps) weapons are mounted. The driver, if there is one, sits at the front surrounded by the drive controls. This concentration of equipment at the front end is a body plan that has evolved independently in such animals as earthworms, crayfish, cockroaches, squid, fish, birds, and mammals. Therefore it must offer many survival advantages. Within vertebrates, it has led to the enlargement of the nerve center in the head, forming the brain. The spinal cord forms the major link between the brain and the rest of the body. Sense organs, for instance the eyes, have developed on the head, providing the shortest possible communications link with the brain. Our brains operate as the body's control center on two main levels. Actions like walking, reading, and memorizing facts involve us 'using' our brains. They are conscious activities. Breathing, beating of the heart, muscular contractions of our intestines, however, are unconscious actions. We cannot control them. The brain directs these actions on 'automatic pilot.' The pituitary gland at the base of the brain, releasing hormones that regulate production of chemical messengers by other glands, also operates automatically.

Scan of a midline section through the head of a healthy 42-year-old woman, showing brain and spinal cord.

The flight and weapons control center of a U.S. Rockwell B-1 bomber aircraft. The bomber is wired with fail-safe offensive and defensive avionics instruments.

❏ The highly folded surface of the cerebrum (the upper, main part) of the human brain, which contains centers responsible for conscious actions and memory, would cover the area of two pages of this book if flattened out.

❏ Electrical activity in the brain is great enough to power a 10-watt lightbulb.

❏ A woman's brain is about 10 percent smaller than a man's, which can vary in weight from 2¼ to 4½lb (1 to 2kg). But brain size and intelligence are not directly related.

In this scan, the red and gold areas are the folds of the cerebral cortex and the cerebellum, the center of balance and coordination. The curved purple area is the corpus callosum, a band of tissue linking the cerebral hemispheres.

The human body's central nervous system. Cranial nerves lead from the base of the brain to all sense organs and facial muscles. Peripheral nerves extend from the spinal cord to all other parts of the body.

❏ The average adult human brain weighs about 3lb (1.4kg). An adult elephant's brain is about four times heavier. The brain of a stegosaur, a dinosaur about the size of a modern elephant, probably weighed less than ½lb (230g).

An illustration of the brain seen in profile, with the spinal cord extending from the base. Dominant are the walnut-like cerebral hemispheres.

Senses and reflexes

Organisms must be aware of changes in their surroundings (stimuli) and respond to these in order to survive. Plants sense variations in light, gravity, touch, and water levels in order to secure light and nutrients. Animals respond to these stimuli as well as to temperature, chemicals, sounds, magnetism, and electricity. This helps them to seek food, shelter, a mate, or to escape injury or enemies. Single-celled organisms and certain plant cells have evolved specialized cellular structures that can detect stimuli and produce a response. The microscopic alga *Chlamydomonas* and the protozoan *Euglena* each have eyespots. These contain the light-sensitive chemical or visual pigment rhodopsin, which also exists in our eyes. The eyespots guide the organisms toward light but away from bright light. When light falls on it, rhodopsin generates an electric current similar to a nerve impulse. This prompts the whip-like flagella on the cells to change their pattern of movement. Among multicellular animals like ourselves, there are external and internal senses. Our eyes, ears, taste buds, nose, and skin respond to stimuli outside the body. Internally, we have stretch receptors on muscles, and neurons sensitive to blood temperature and carbon dioxide levels. Together these play a role in maintaining stable conditions within the body. Like many creatures, we also have a system of quick, automatic responses to dangers. These are known as reflex actions. Swallowing, coughing, blinking, and withdrawing one's hand from a fire, are all examples of these. We do them without thinking.

Guard cells that surround stomata, the tiny breathing pores in leaf surfaces, like these on a *Mimosa* leaf, are sensitive to moisture changes in air.

With reflex action, muscles of the iris make the pupil of the eye bigger in dim light, smaller in bright light.

Touch a snail's soft body and, as a reflex action, it withdraws into its protective shell.

Go to strike someone on the head and they will automatically blink to prevent damage to their eyes. But it is possible to stop oneself blinking. Consciously one can override this reflex action.

Put to the breast, a baby automatically seeks out the nipple to take milk. Reflex actions are controlled by the autonomic nervous system, a network separate from the central nervous system.

❏ Russian biologist Ivan Pavlov persuaded dogs to produce digestive juices not on sight of food – the normal reflex action – but just on seeing the food bowl or even in response to a flashing light. Pavlov 'reprogrammed' the dogs' automatic eating response. His experiments gave rise to the phrase 'a Pavlovian response,' which refers to a behavioral reaction that has been conditioned by this sort of programming.

❏ Insects such as moths move toward a source of light while others, for example cockroaches and woodlice, move away from it. A moth's response to light is so great that it will fly into the flame of a candle, where it is instantly burnt to death.

❏ Like homing pigeons that can find their way back to their lofts in darkness over distances of hundreds of miles, humans that have been blindfolded and transported many miles from a release point have been able to indicate the direction of home accurately and without fail. Pigeons and humans seem to have a sixth sense – the ability to navigate using the Earth's magnetic field as a guide.

❏ Deciduous trees such as the oak, chestnut, and sycamore 'sense' the onset of winter. They shed their leaves in the fall to avoid excess loss of water and damage from frost and snow.

Cellular vision – the multifaceted eye

A mosaic is created by carefully piecing together a multitude of separate units, or cells.

The head of a Black fly, with its multifaceted, or compound, eyes colored gold. The eyes are especially sensitive to moving objects as these trigger each of the visual units.

The Ancient Romans were famous for their mosaics – pictures and designs composed of many small pieces of stone, tile, or glass. The images perceived by animals such as insects, crabs, and lobsters, resemble mosaics. An insect's eye, for instance, consists of thousands of identical visual units. Each has a lens or facet that focuses light on to a transparent rod. Receptor cells around the rod are stimulated to fire nerve impulses to the brain. The units record the presence or absence of light, light intensity and, by their position on the eye, the direction of incoming light. Together they form an image made up of many dots. If we look at a mosaic close-up we can distinguish the individual fragments of stone. From a distance, though, the fragments seem to blend together. This phenomenon is largely the basis for the 'visual trickery' we play on ourselves in producing television, newspaper printing, and computer images. All of these create mosaic images but our eyes cannot normally perceive the individual dots. This is because movements of the head and the action of eye muscles produces a constant vibration of the eyes that blurs the dots. Or the pattern of dots on a television screen changes so rapidly that we cannot fix on the tiny pinpricks of light.

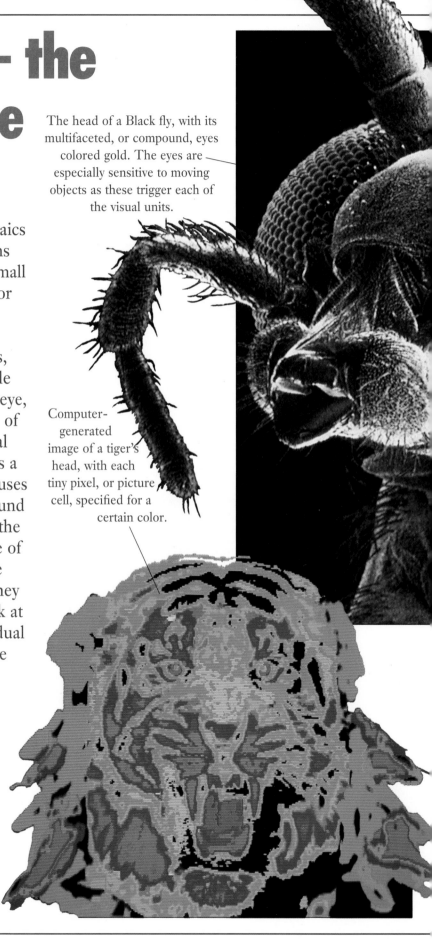

Computer-generated image of a tiger's head, with each tiny pixel, or picture cell, specified for a certain color.

A fly's eyes each have about 5,000 optical units.

The compound eyes of insects and many shellfish cover most of the 360 degrees of field of view surrounding the animals.

Insect eyes can detect polarized light, which shows the position of the Sun.

The Multiple Mirror Telescope on Mount Hopkins, Arizona. It consists of six 72in (1.8m) diameter mirrors which together work like a single telescope.

A cluster of facets on a Bluebottle fly's eye, magnified ×400. Each facet cell sends signals to the brain, which constructs a mosaic image.

❏ A fly's compound eye would need to be about 3ft (90cm) in diameter to create images as clear and detailed as can be perceived by the human eye.

❏ Dragonflies have two sets of eyes, one simple, the other compound. The simple eyes are sensitive to the difference between direct and reflected sunlight. They allow the flies to distinguish between the sky and the ground and so help them fly on a level course. Each compound eye contains over 25,000 visual units and forms a mosaic image.

❏ If we were able to keep our eyes perfectly still, we would probably see nothing at all. The light-sensitive cells of the retina only respond to changing levels of light. A constant level overstimulates them and they do not fire messages.

❏ The pattern of dots forming images printed in books and newspapers consists of between 3,000 and 40,000 dots per square inch (6.25cm^2).

Seeing things in black and white or color

Sunlight appears to be colorless. We often call it white light. But it is really a mixture of many colors or wavelengths. (Light travels in waves like the ripples created when you throw a stone in a pond. The distance between the tops of successive ripples is known as the wavelength.) You can see the various colors of light when a rainbow appears in the sky after heavy rain. White light is split by raindrops acting as prisms into bands of red, orange, yellow, green, blue, indigo, and violet. Different creatures respond to one or more of these wavelengths depending on the light-sensitive chemicals or visual pigments they possess. Plants and algae, for example, contain chlorophyll and carotene, which absorb violet and red, or blue and green wavelengths respectively. Animals have similar pigments in their eyespots or eyes. Our own eyes contain two types of light receptors, rods and cones. Rods can only detect shades of gray. They equip us for night vision. Cones are for day vision and can distinguish colors. Some contain a pigment sensitive to red light, some to blue light, and others to green. According to the types and numbers of cones stimulated by light entering the eyes, the brain receives an impression of color.

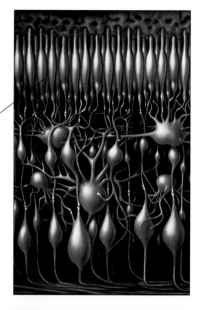

Illustration of the layers of nerve cells in the retina of the eye. Rods outnumber cones 20:1, hence only rods are shown here.

Anatomy of the eyes with, on the right, the front of the eyeball dissected and shown in detail.

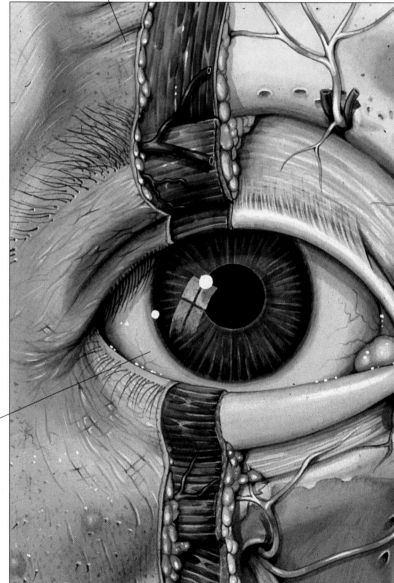

The white of the eyeball is the outer coat of tough, fibrous tissue with the transparent cornea in front.

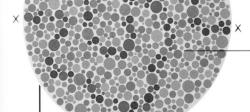

A color blindness test. People unable to distinguish between red and green will not see a pathway of green dots between the two X marks, only hues of red.

Bees see in color as we do, but are also sensitive to ultraviolet light. Many flowers have evolved ultraviolet markings that guide bees to their nectar sources.

The cornea, lens, and aqueous humour, the fluid in the front section of the eye, refract, or bend, light rays and bring them to a focus on the retina. Muscles linked to the lens relax or contract to alter its curvature and hence refractive powers.

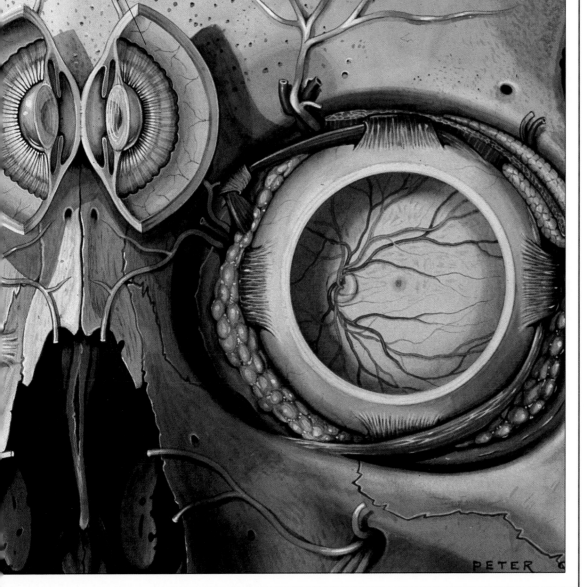

PETER

FACT FILE

❑ Each of our eyes contain approximately 125 million rods and 7 million cones.

❑ Birds such as eagles have even better color vision than us. They have not three but five visual pigments, and some have eye filters that can cut out glare like polarized sunglasses.

❑ Perfect vision – opticians record this as 20:20 (or 6:6) vision – refers to the ability to read letters 1/3rd of an inch (8.5mm) tall on a card placed 20ft (6m) away. The letters create an image on the retina only 1/1,000th of an inch (0.025mm) high.

❑ When we look at an object, each of our eyes sends a set of impulses to the brain, where they are interpreted as a single image. Drinking too much alcohol upsets this interpretation and we see double or blurred images.

On the right wavelength

The atmosphere is awash with waves – sound waves, radio waves, infrared rays, gamma rays, X-rays, and so on. Most of these we cannot detect. We are sensitive to sound waves, though, which we perceive with our ears. Sound waves are vibrations of the air, a form of pressure waves. The vibrations set our ear drums in motion and the tiny bones in our ears, the ossicles, amplify and transmit the sound waves to sensory cells within the cochlea of each ear. The cochlea is a spiral of fluid-filled canals from which nerves lead to the auditory, or hearing, centers of the brain. Although we live in a world filled with sound waves, our ears are tuned in to only a limited range of them in the same way that a radio can pick up, say, either long-, medium- or short-wave signals. We can detect frequencies of from 20 to 20,000 waves a second. We use sounds for communication. Bats, which use sounds for navigation and hunting, are sensitive to sounds of 120,000 waves a second. Sound waves travel better through water than through air, and fish and sea mammals are especially adapted to detect them. Whales emit a variety of sounds for communication and navigation underwater.

These Fennec foxes, night-time hunters of desert areas in North Africa and the Middle East, have especially large ears to detect prey by sounds. The ears also act as radiators to disperse excess body heat.

This Bull shark locates its prey using its lateral line system, an array of pressure-sensitive units just below its skin.

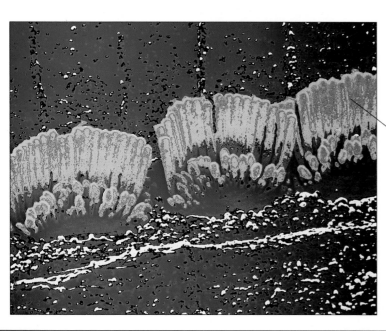

Rows of hair cells in the cochlea of the ear, ×3,500 magnification. Sound waves mechanically stimulate the hairs, which send impulses to the auditory centers of the brain.

Bats echolocate, sending out sound waves produced in the larynx and projected from the nose. Their ears detect any waves bouncing back from an object, providing information about its size and proximity.

A Bechstein's bat closes in on its insect prey, which it scoops up in its wings then brings to the mouth.

The top of British Telecom Tower in London is festooned with dish aerials for receiving and relaying telephone and radio signals.

It's in the balance

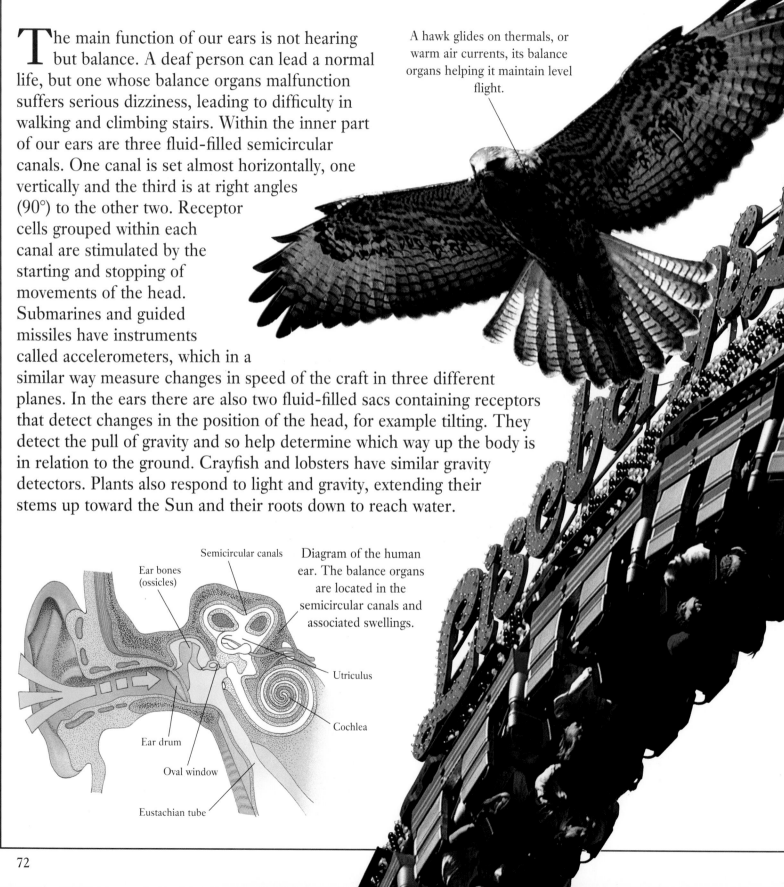

The main function of our ears is not hearing but balance. A deaf person can lead a normal life, but one whose balance organs malfunction suffers serious dizziness, leading to difficulty in walking and climbing stairs. Within the inner part of our ears are three fluid-filled semicircular canals. One canal is set almost horizontally, one vertically and the third is at right angles (90°) to the other two. Receptor cells grouped within each canal are stimulated by the starting and stopping of movements of the head. Submarines and guided missiles have instruments called accelerometers, which in a similar way measure changes in speed of the craft in three different planes. In the ears there are also two fluid-filled sacs containing receptors that detect changes in the position of the head, for example tilting. They detect the pull of gravity and so help determine which way up the body is in relation to the ground. Crayfish and lobsters have similar gravity detectors. Plants also respond to light and gravity, extending their stems up toward the Sun and their roots down to reach water.

A hawk glides on thermals, or warm air currents, its balance organs helping it maintain level flight.

Semicircular canals

Ear bones (ossicles)

Diagram of the human ear. The balance organs are located in the semicircular canals and associated swellings.

Utriculus

Cochlea

Ear drum

Oval window

Eustachian tube

Inside the statocysts, the balance organs of this shrimp, are sand grains. The grains move as the animal swims or walks, and stimulate any sensory hairs that they touch.

Composite image of an aircraft and an air traffic control screen. To avoid collisions, aircraft are designated different heights, speeds, and flight paths, and their automatic pilots are programmed with this data.

Riding on a rollercoaster. As the body is accelerated forward, turned upside-down, and pulled one way then the other, receptor cells in the semicircular canals and utriculus of the ear are stimulated. They relay messages to the balance and posture centers in the cerebellum, midbrain, and spinal cord.

Electrical and temperature sensitivity

Demonstration of magnetic levitation and the link between temperature and electrical resistance. A ceramic plate, cooled by liquid nitrogen, becomes superconducting so current continues to flow and the plate is magnetic even when power is cut off. The plate repels a magnet placed above it.

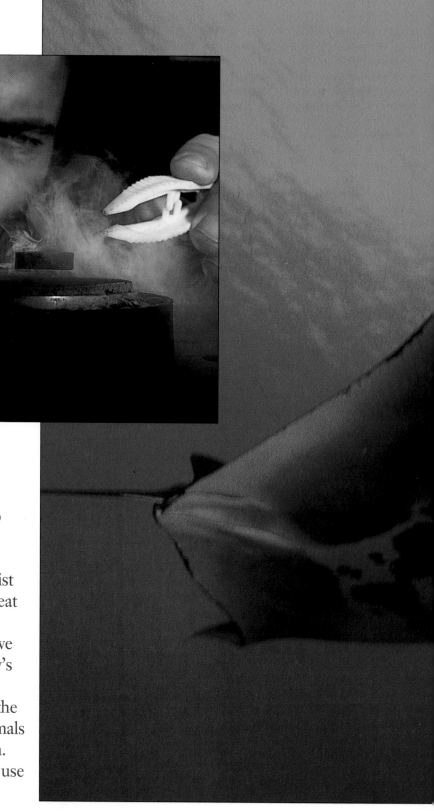

Sharks, rays, and many other predatory fish can detect the tiny amounts of electricity produced by a prey's muscles and nerves as it moves and breathes. They can sense electric fields of only a thousandth of a volt over distances of up to 3ft (1m). Among mammals, only the Duckbill platypus of Australia seems to have an electrical sense. It, too, uses it to detect its prey (shrimps) in the water. Its electroreceptors lie within its bill. All mammals, however, have temperature receptors. These consist of nerve endings in the skin that are sensitive to heat and cold. Mammals – and all other vertebrates – possess a hypothalamus, a part of the brain sensitive to fluctuations in blood temperature. It is the body's thermostat. Snakes and bats have the most sophisticated heat sensors. These are situated on the head and are used to locate prey. Birds and mammals give off body heat in the form of infrared radiation. Rattlesnakes and vampire bats can detect this and use it to build up a 'picture' of their victims.

Germination of a Broad bean seed. Root tip cells are sensitive to gravity, moisture, chemical and electrical fields.

Thermographs of a man, woman, and child – computer-enhanced images showing heat emitted by the body. White is the hottest, and blue and purple the coldest parts.

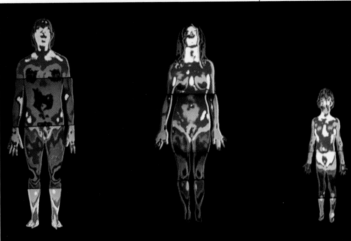

A Manta ray, a fish that can detect weak electrical currents in water. It uses this ability to locate animals living buried in sand on the sea bottom, notably flatfish on which it preys.

The Mallee fowl of Australia prepares a mound of rotting vegetable matter in which it will bury its eggs for incubation. If the mound temperature drops, the bird piles on more vegetation.

Sense of smell

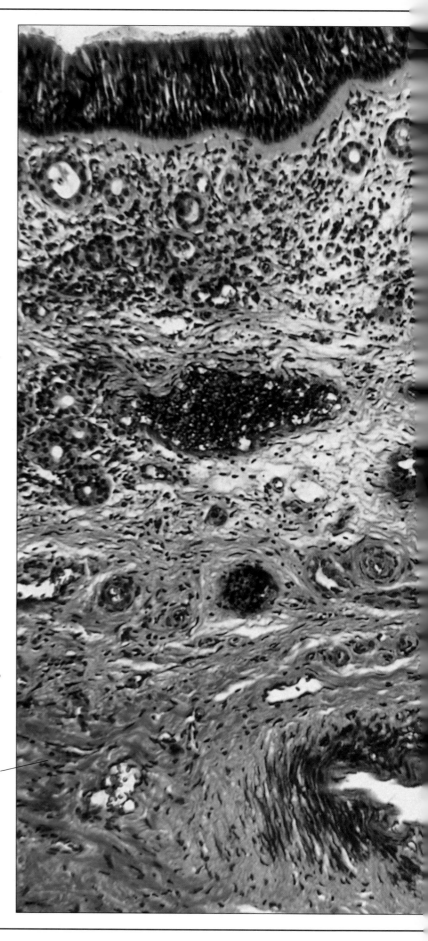

S mell and taste both involve a sensitivity to chemicals. For land animals, smell is a response to chemicals carried in air currents and it functions over large distances. Taste is only perceived when chemicals make contact with receptor cells. For creatures living in water, the distinction between smell and taste is blurred. Compared to most vertebrates, our sense of smell is not good. Yet we can discriminate up to 4,000 different odors. Receptor cells inside the nose bear long hair-like cilia that are embedded in mucus. Chemicals must dissolve in the mucus in order to fire the smell receptors. We seem to have between 7 and 15 different kinds of smell receptor. Each responds to a specific type of chemical. Different odors and scents stimulate one or more of the receptors and to varying degrees. Dogs, with their acute sense of smell, have up to 30 types of smell receptor and each is 1 million times more sensitive than our own. This is why we often use dogs to track people, foxes, badgers, and even to hunt out drugs and explosives.

This Brown trout finds its way back to its home waters using its sense of taste, detecting the chemical signature of the water.

Section through the lining of the nasal cavity where the olfactory cells (purple) form a continuous surface layer.

A girl sniffs the scent from a tulip flower. The petals produce a chemical messenger that attracts bees and other large insects.

❏ When a bee stings, it releases an alarm scent that attracts others nearby to join in the attack. Like other insects, bees smell primarily with the antennae on their heads, but they also have smell receptors on their mouthparts and legs.

❏ A major ingredient of perfumes is musk. This is a pungent jelly-like oily liquid made by male Musk deer to mark their home areas.

A Polar bear sniffs the ground in search of a whiff of blood from an injured prey, which is usually a Ringed seal.

This layer is connective tissue, containing nerve fibers, glands, and blood vessels.

The inside of the nasal cavity. The olfactory membrane is covered in mucus. Nerve fibers lead from the sensory cells to the olfactory bulb which relays smell signals to the brain.

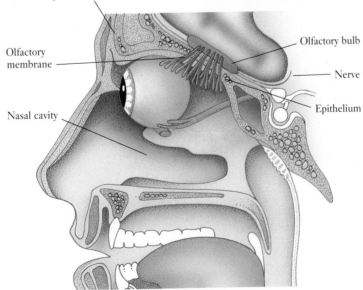

Olfactory membrane

Nasal cavity

Olfactory bulb

Nerve

Epithelium

❏ In the Perigord region of France, pigs are used to find and dig up truffles, which are large fungi eaten as delicacies. Female pigs – sows – are used. They sniff out the truffles, growing up to 15in (37.5cm) below ground, which seem to give off a smell similar to the sexually stimulating chemicals produced by the male or boar.

❏ The smell-sensitive lining of our noses contains more than 10 million receptor cells.

Bitter-sweetness, flavors and taste

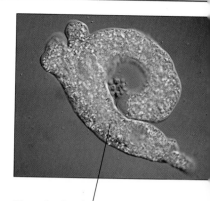

Even lowly *Amoeba*-like creatures such as this one engulfing a cluster of tiny green oval cells, seem to have a taste preference.

A winetaster takes a good mouthful of wine, not a sip, and swills it around to let it reach every part of the mouth. This is to allow the wine to come in contact with the different sorts of taste-buds on the tongue and those scattered at the back of the throat. We can distinguish only four types of taste – sweet, sour, salt, and bitter. Our perception of taste is a combination of these together with sensory information about the smell, texture, and temperature of the test substance. Smell affects flavor because odors freely pass from the mouth to the nasal chamber via passages within the skull. The tongue is covered with about 3,000 taste buds containing chemical receptors. These are up to 10,000 times less sensitive than the receptors in the nose. But then taste is not such an important sense for us. It is, though, for most aquatic animals. They use taste to navigate and to find food and mates. They can detect the source and nature of different chemicals carried in currents from riverbanks, beaches, and from all sorts of plants and other animals.

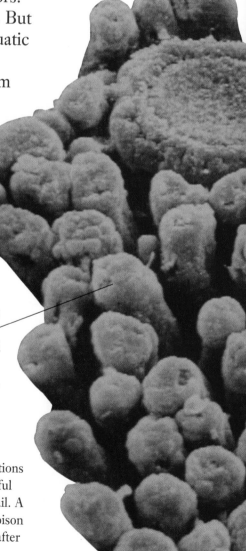

Not the surface of a planet but of the human tongue, magnified ×60. Embedded within these tiny projections, called papillae, are the taste buds.

Attempts to kill pest populations of Brown rats with powerful poisons like cyanide often fail. A rat that gets a taste of the poison but does not die, will thereafter avoid poisoned bait.

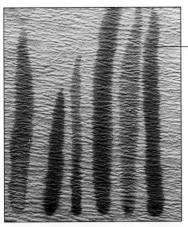

The chemical constituents of foodstuffs that stimulate our taste buds can be identified by chromatography – dissolving them in a solvent and observing the distance each moves along a filter paper.

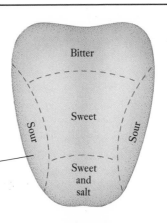

The various areas of the human tongue have taste buds responding to one of four different primary flavors.

Bitter

Sweet

Sour

Sour

Sweet and salt

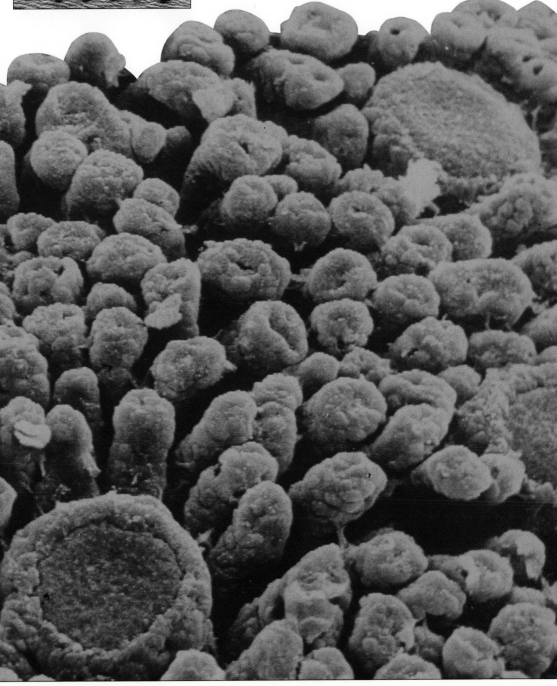

❏ Moths and butterflies have taste sensors on their feet. These are sensitive to water, salt, or sugar.

❏ Pigs have twice as many taste buds on their tongues as we do.

❏ Fish have the most highly developed taste system. They have taste buds not only on the tongue but also scattered over the surface of the body.

❏ Red peppers and curries taste 'hot' not just because they stimulate the taste buds in a unique way but also because they fire general nerve endings on the lips, cheeks, and roof of the mouth.

❏ The sight, smell, and taste of food stimulates the automatic secretion of saliva from glands in the mouth. This ensures that digestion of food by enzymes in saliva can take place in the few seconds that food remains in the mouth before being swallowed.

❏ To stimulate our taste buds, food particles must be dissolved in saliva or in secretions from special glands within the tongue. We have taste buds in our throats – on the pharynx, epiglottis, and the larynx – as well as on the tongue. Nerve signals pass from these to the taste centers on the surface of the cerebral hemispheres of the brain.

Touch sensors

Roots produce thousands of root hairs for absorption of minerals and water. As these encounter soil particles, they grow in a new direction.

All animals have tactile or touch-sensitive hairs on the surface of the body to detect contact with objects. At the bases of these are receptors that are fired as the hairs become bent. Many invertebrates automatically withdraw their bodies on being touched: earthworms, sea anemones, and woodlice are examples of creatures that react like this. Social insects – ants, bees, wasps, and termites – communicate with one another by touch. We have a range of tactile receptors, embedded in the skin and deep within the body. Some of those in the skin respond to steady pressure, some to sudden deformations such as a pinprick, and others to pain. Together they provide information about the shape, texture, and weight of objects. Proprioreceptors are special internal touch-sensitive nerve endings that monitor the stretch of muscles and the presence of food in the stomach, urine in the bladder, and a fetus in the woman's uterus. They play a part in muscular coordination and general body self-awareness. There are also internal pain receptors. These give a warning of injury. However, the sense of pain is imprecise. A pinprick can cause as much pain as a broken bone.

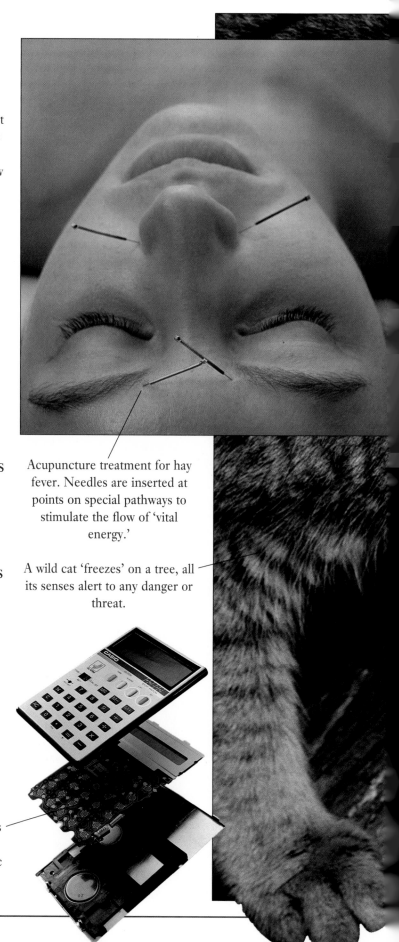

Acupuncture treatment for hay fever. Needles are inserted at points on special pathways to stimulate the flow of 'vital energy.'

A wild cat 'freezes' on a tree, all its senses alert to any danger or threat.

Exploded view of a pocket calculator showing control circuitry beneath the keypad. As a button is pressed, the circuit beneath is closed and an electric current flows to the central processing unit.

Diagrammatic section of the human skin showing a touch-sensitive hair and various nerve endings sensitive to continuous pressure, pinprick-like touch, stretching, and texture.

Wild animals' whiskers are often longer than those of their domestic relatives – an adaptation to constant nighttime hunting.

A Black-tailed godwit probes for food in the shallows of a lake. It has touch-sensitive nerve endings on its long beak.

❏ Touch receptors in the ears of pigeons are sensitive to subtle changes in atmospheric pressure. The birds may use this information to determine their altitude in flight and, like a barometer, to foresee changes in the weather.

❏ In mammals, sensitivity to touch is increased by the presence of bristles or whiskers, which act as extensions of the body. They are important for animals that are active at night (nocturnal), like cats and civets, or in those that swim in murky waters, for instance otters, dugongs, and hippopotamuses.

❏ Seals seem to rely more on touch information from their whiskers than on sight to home in and catch fish to eat.

❏ Water striders can sense tiny ripples on the surface of water with tactile sensors on their legs. The insects thus locate their predators (fish, frogs, caddis larvae) and their prey (midges).

❏ Human touch receptors are most numerous on the tips of fingers, toes, the penis and clitoris, and on the tongue.

❏ From birth, some people suffer a rare disorder which leaves them without the sensation of pain. But while they do not experience the pain of a toothache or the prick of a needle, they are in constant danger of injuries of which they are not aware.

Similarity or variety – strategies for survival

A sea of tulips with some daffodils, two species of flowering plant. A species is defined as a group of similar organisms whose members can breed with one another to produce fertile offspring.

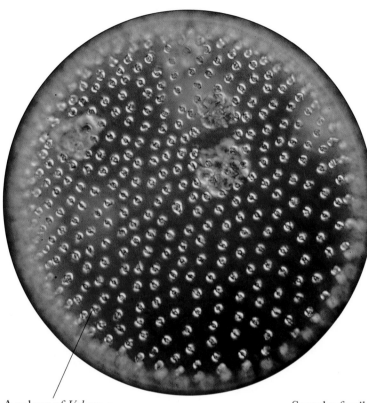

A colony of *Volvox*, a single-celled creature that reproduces both asexually and sexually. Growing within this parent colony are six 'daughter' colonies.

Spot the family resemblance? Each person acquires a mixture of characteristics from both mother and father when sperm fertilizes egg or ovum.

Living things can reproduce in two ways: asexually and sexually. With the asexual method, offspring are produced without the fusion of sex cells – sperm and eggs. It usually involves the body splitting in half. The offspring are all identical to the parent. Sexual reproduction involves the mixing of genes – the hereditary material (see overleaf) – from two parents. It produces offspring that are different from their parents. Each method has its own survival advantages, and some creatures can use one method or the other depending on the environment or the stages in their life cycle. Many simple creatures reproduce asexually when they reach a certain size. Among flowering plants, the production of bulbs, corms, tubers, and rhizomes is an asexual process. In sexual reproduction, the fusion of sperm and eggs is known as fertilization, and its product is called an embryo or zygote. We shall look in detail at these processes, and their variations, on the following eight pages of the book.

These ripe peas are the result of successful fertilization.

Not two, but seven peas in a pod. While the peas look identical, genetically they are unique. Each ovule in the pod was fertilized by a different pollen grain.

Chemical blueprint for life

The appearance and much of the behavior of living things is determined by a chemical known as deoxyribonucleic acid, or DNA for short. It contains a code, the genetic code, which controls the manufacture of specific proteins in cells. As building units, enzymes, antibodies, and carriers of oxygen, proteins are essential for life. A molecule of DNA is like a spiral staircase or twisted ladder. Its structure is often called a double helix. A related chemical, ribonucleic acid, or RNA for short, resembles half of this – a long strand with half-rungs. The genetic code is made up of a series of triplets of half-rungs (bases) known as codons. RNA acts as a go-between, reading the code on DNA and translating it into sequences of chemicals (amino acids) that make up different proteins. Random changes in DNA, known as mutations, produce new genetic blueprints and hence variety with living things. Mutations occur naturally in about one in every 200,000 chances. Some individuals become better suited to their environment than others and this determines their chances of survival and producing offspring.

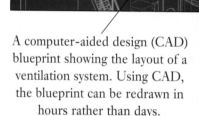

A computer-aided design (CAD) blueprint showing the layout of a ventilation system. Using CAD, the blueprint can be redrawn in hours rather than days.

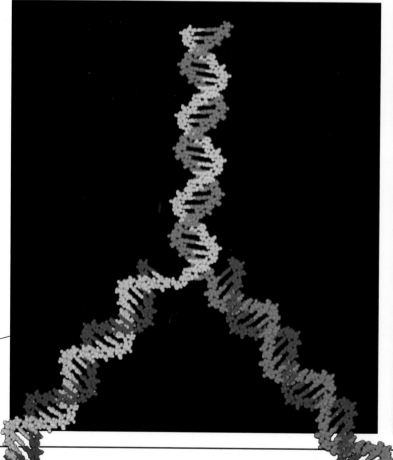

Schematic representation of the replication of DNA. As the two interwoven strands of the parent molecule (above) unwind, each acts as a template for the growth of new strands (shown in purple).

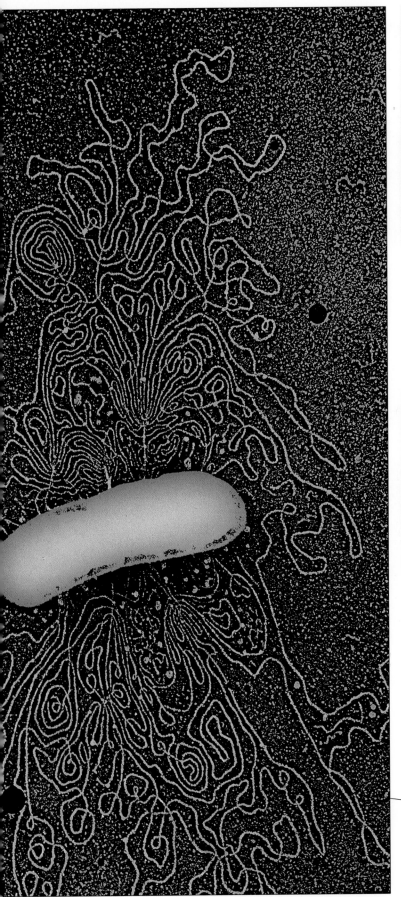

Examining the chemical composition of DNA from a parasitic worm. Each group of four strips represents the sequence of the DNA bases.

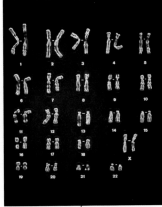

The nucleus of each human cell, except sperm and ova, contains 46 chromosomes, here set out as 22 pairs and the sex chromosomes (XX for female, XY for male).

A thread of DNA (gold) spews from an *Escherischia coli*, a bacterial cell. The cell was treated so that its wall burst. *E. coli* is much used in biotechnology since DNA from other organisms can be inserted into its own DNA and 'switched on' to produce non-bacterial products.

❏ In DNA there are 4 types of code units (bases) and 64 possible codons. A strand of DNA may contain hundreds of codons and these can be arranged in any order, with some repeated and others not present. The number of possible different sequences runs into billions.

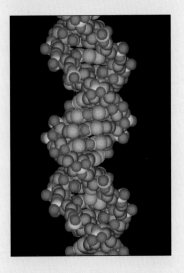

❏ The structure of DNA was discovered in 1953 in Cambridge University, England, by molecular biologists James Watson of the U.S.A. and Francis Crick of England. They received a joint Nobel Prize in Medicine, along with another English scientist, Maurice Wilkins, for this discovery in 1962. They used the term 'The Double Helix' to describe DNA's spiral structure.

❏ DNA molecules are large, containing up to 10 million atoms. But within cells they are so highly folded and coiled that they take up only 1/10,000th of their unwound length and are invisible to the naked eye.

Simple cell division and cloning

In simple creatures such as bacteria, yeasts and *Amoeba,* reproduction occurs as part of growth. As cells reach a certain size they split in half. This is called cell fission. It produces clones of cells – genetically identical copies of the parent. In more complex living things, cloning is the basis of growth. Our own bodies are largely composed of clones of nerve, muscle, blood, bone cells and so on that formed from a few cells of the early embryo. However, the cloning of whole human beings remains a topic for science fiction – although perhaps not for long. Clones of mice, frogs, sheep, and cows have already been produced. To do this, the cells of a tiny embryo are separated. The nucleus (containing the genetic blueprint) from each one is inserted singly into single-cell embryos from which the nuclei have been removed. The man-made embryos with identical nuclei are placed in the wombs of females, where they develop into youngsters. To clone people in this way is biologically feasible.

A mother zebra and her young. Endangered wild animals are now bred in captivity, sometimes by using foster mothers for preserved embryos. The embryos can be made by splitting the ball of cells that forms following fertilization, in which case the embryos are clones.

A freshwater coelenterate, *Hydra,* with a clone about to 'bud off' the side and with small bumps containing sex cells to be released.

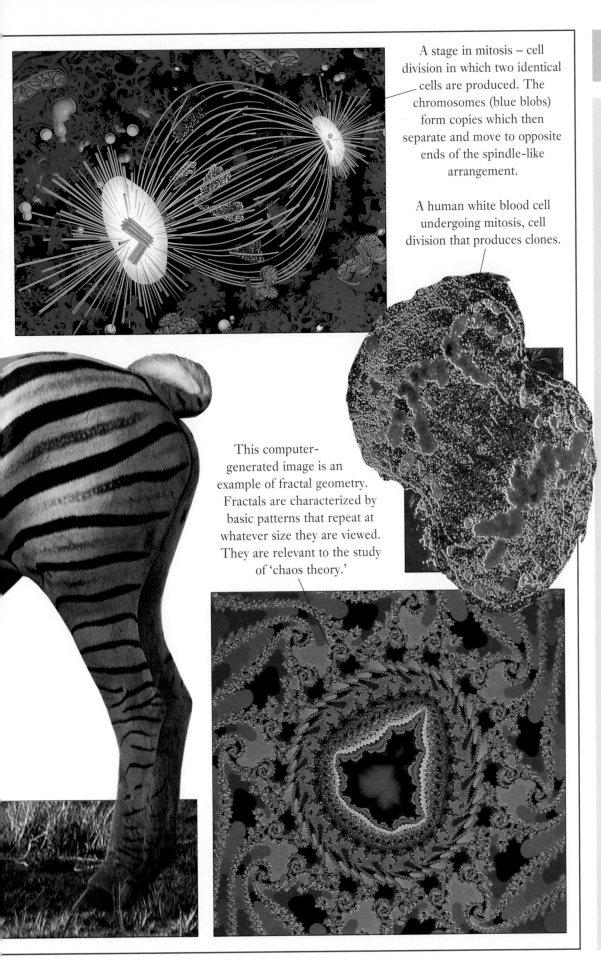

A stage in mitosis – cell division in which two identical cells are produced. The chromosomes (blue blobs) form copies which then separate and move to opposite ends of the spindle-like arrangement.

A human white blood cell undergoing mitosis, cell division that produces clones.

This computer-generated image is an example of fractal geometry. Fractals are characterized by basic patterns that repeat at whatever size they are viewed. They are relevant to the study of 'chaos theory.'

❏ For centuries gardeners have been making clones of plants. The cuttings of shoots from a rose bush that on insertion in soil develop into new plants have the same genetic make-up as the parent.

❏ When flatworms divide asexually their bodies do not simply split in half but the head end gets about 75 percent of the body and tail the rest. The head end becomes fully grown in days, the tail end in weeks.

❏ Genetic engineers have artifically produced clones of human cells that help fight infections. Hybridoma cells are combinations of antibody-producing white blood cells and special cancer cells from mice. Unlike the normal white cells, they produce only one type of antibody, known as monoclonal antibodies.

❏ Given ideal conditions, a bacterial cell can reproduce by cell fission once every 20 minutes. By the end of a day, it can give rise to a population of tens of millions of billions of cells.

❏ In May 1987, the last known individual of the Dusky seaside sparrow died at Disney World, Florida, U.S.A. Some of its tissues have been frozen in the hope that one day it will be possible to produce clones of the species from single cells. To date, clones have only been produced from embryo cells, which have not yet developed (differentiated) into tissue cells.

Virgin birth

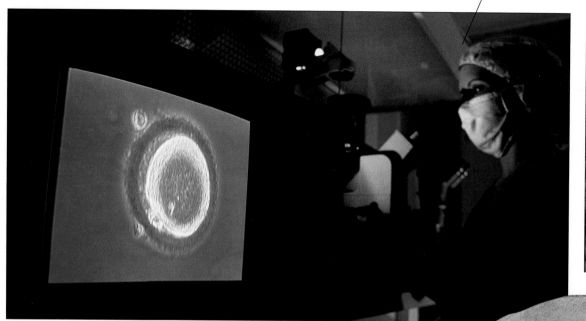

Examining a microscope image of a human ovum for fertilization in a test tube and perhaps, in future, for parthenogenesis.

An eland has given birth to a bongo, a related species of antelope. A bongo embryo was transferred into the uterus of the foster mother eland.

Virgin birth or parthenogenesis is a special type of sexual reproduction in which individuals develop from unfertilized eggs. Sperm cells are rarely involved, and there is no mixing of genetic material. It is performed by plants and such animals as insects, fish, and reptiles. There is no conclusive evidence for human virgin birth. Yet the eggs of frogs and rabbits, which also do not undergo parthenogenesis naturally, can be made to develop without fertilization by treating them with various chemicals or pricking them with a fine needle. Virgin birth usually occurs in species that lead a precarious life, for example where the chances of finding a sexual partner are slim or where supplies of food are unpredictable. Its advantages include the ability to produce offspring rapidly and to control the numbers of male and females being reproduced. A queen bee, for instance, can select whether or not to allow sperm to fertilize her eggs. The fertilized ones give rise to females, workers, and other queens, while eggs that develop parthenogenetically become males (drones). A queen bee mates only once in her life. She stores sperm in her body to use as and when required.

A test tube with human sperm and ova is to be placed in an incubator where fertilization may occur. Potential mothers are given fertility drugs to stimulate production of several ova.

A Honey bee colony. One male bee does most of the breeding in the hive, which leads to some individuals having more than 50 percent of their genetic material in common.

The bongo baby has the characteristics of its parents and acquires no genetic material from the foster mother, only parental care.

❏ Rotifers are microscopic aquatic worms also called wheel animals. Sometimes the females reproduce other females by virgin birth. Then they produce eggs some of which develop into males and others into eggs needing fertilization by sperm from those males.

❏ The Central American fish *Mollienisia formosa* produces eggs that do not need to be fertilized to develop into embryos but do require sperm cells to make contact with them. The sperm can be from any of several species of fish.

❏ The life cycle of animals such as aphids, or greenfly, involves phases of sexual reproduction followed by phases of virgin birth.

❏ The offspring of virgin birth in humans would almost certainly be female. Within our genetic blueprint there is different information (the sex chromosomes) for a male and female. Female cells can only give rise to other female cells.

Sperm and egg

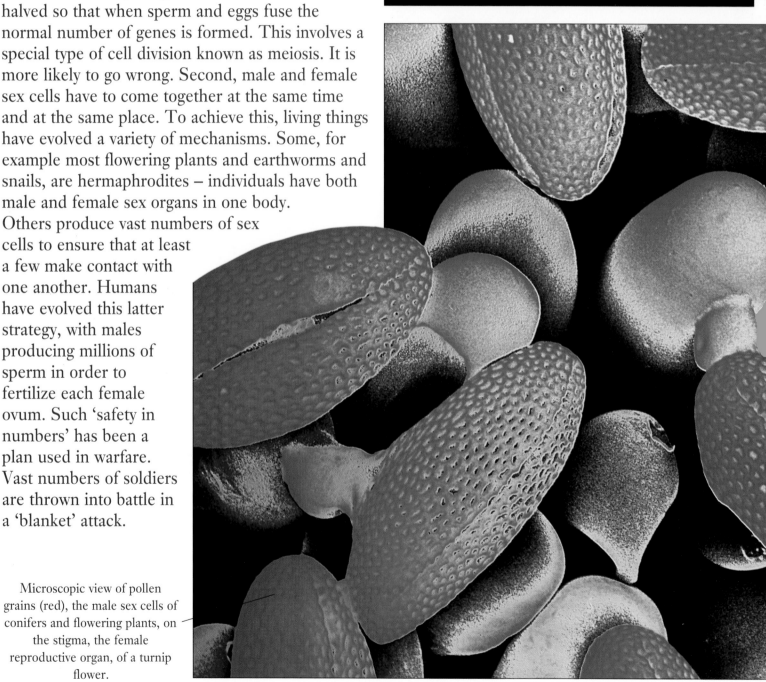

Sex makes the world go around, but not without problems. The great advantage of sexual reproduction is that it allows mixing of genes so that good mutations can increase in a population and bad ones can be eliminated. The disadvantages are twofold. First, the genetic material must be halved so that when sperm and eggs fuse the normal number of genes is formed. This involves a special type of cell division known as meiosis. It is more likely to go wrong. Second, male and female sex cells have to come together at the same time and at the same place. To achieve this, living things have evolved a variety of mechanisms. Some, for example most flowering plants and earthworms and snails, are hermaphrodites – individuals have both male and female sex organs in one body. Others produce vast numbers of sex cells to ensure that at least a few make contact with one another. Humans have evolved this latter strategy, with males producing millions of sperm in order to fertilize each female ovum. Such 'safety in numbers' has been a plan used in warfare. Vast numbers of soldiers are thrown into battle in a 'blanket' attack.

Microscopic view of pollen grains (red), the male sex cells of conifers and flowering plants, on the stigma, the female reproductive organ, of a turnip flower.

Computer-colored image of a human sperm. The head region (green) contains the 23 chromosomes of the male sex cell. The whiplike tail is packed with mitochondria (pink), the cell's powerhouses.

Illustration of the moment of fertilization of a mammal's egg by a single sperm. Competing sperm are blocked at the surface.

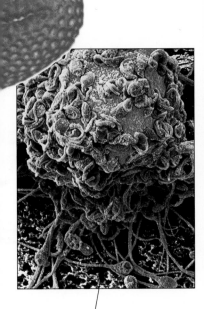

Human sperm (pale brown) surrounding a human ovum. One sperm will penetrate the ovum wall and fuse with the nucleus.

A collection of eggs of the dinosaur *Protoceratops*, found in the Gobi Desert.

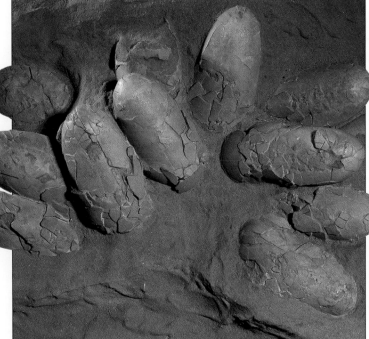

❑ In her lifetime, a female plaice will produce about 20 million eggs. On average only two or three of these will develop and the young reach maturity and breed.

❑ On a birch tree, each male catkin can produce more than 5 million pollen grains (the 'sperm' of flowering plants). There are several thousand such catkins on a fully grown birch so at least some pollen stands a chance of being blown by the wind on to female catkins and fertilizing the ova.

❑ During human sexual intercourse, the man places up to 200 million sperm inside the woman's uterus to try and fertilize just one ovum. They swim at a speed of about ½in (1.2cm) a minute toward the ovum. Size for size, that is about the speed of an Olympic swimming champion.

❑ The sex life of certain orchids depends on their flowers looking, smelling, and feeling like the females of insects such as bees and wasps. The male insects land on the flowers and accidentally pick up pollen. When they visit another flower, this becomes deposited on female structures of the flowers. The transfer of pollen from male to female parts of flowers is called pollination.

Taking shape, becoming organized

Minutes after an egg or ovum is fertilized, it divides and starts to develop into a multicellular ball. This first stage in a creature's life, when it is featureless and usually incapable of survival on its own, is known as the embryo. Within a few days the embryo's genetic blueprint begins to program the formation of different types of cell. Various genes are switched on and off to establish the shape, form, and functioning of each cell. The cells migrate to different parts of the expanding ball and form clones. Tissues develop, organs form, and the body starts to take on its final shape. The embryo is transformed into an independent creature. In plants and in birds, most insects, and aquatic invertebrates, the fertilized egg is supplied with all the food resources the growing embryo will need. In sharks, lizards, and some insects and snakes, the embryos are self-sufficient in food but the female keeps the eggs inside her body until the young are well-developed. In mammals, the fertilized eggs are provisioned with food from the mother until the young are able to live alone, as we describe overleaf.

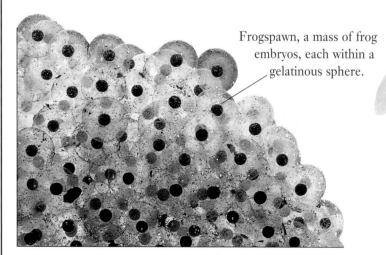

Frogspawn, a mass of frog embryos, each within a gelatinous sphere.

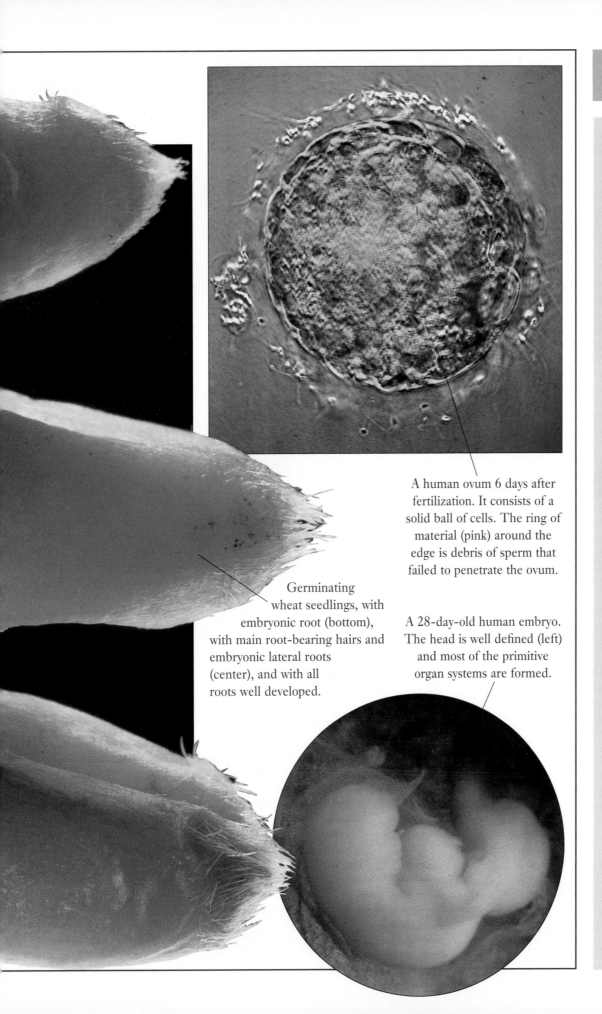

A human ovum 6 days after fertilization. It consists of a solid ball of cells. The ring of material (pink) around the edge is debris of sperm that failed to penetrate the ovum.

Germinating wheat seedlings, with embryonic root (bottom), with main root-bearing hairs and embryonic lateral roots (center), and with all roots well developed.

A 28-day-old human embryo. The head is well defined (left) and most of the primitive organ systems are formed.

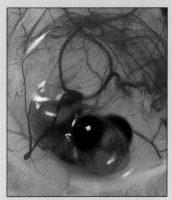

Pregnancy and the fetus

One of your father's sperm met one of your mother's eggs (or ova) high up in one of her fallopian tubes and fertilization occurred. About 30 hours later, the first cell division of the ovum took place. By the time the developing embryo (you!) reached her uterus, 2 to 6 days later, it consisted of a ball of 32 cells. This embedded itself in the wall of the uterus and here it remained, constantly growing, until you were born some 9 months later. As an embryo, you received food and oxygen from your mother's blood supply via the placenta and umbilical cord, and you were protected from everyday knocks and bumps by the fluid-filled amniotic sac. All placental mammals – ourselves, cats, dogs, rabbits, monkeys and the like – start life in this way. Marsupials are mammals in which the young are born at a very early stage of development and then fed on milk from their mother within a pouch on her belly. They include kangaroos, wallabies, and possums. The duck-billed platypus and echidnas are mammals that lay eggs like reptiles and birds, but then feed the young on milk in the same way that we do.

A human embryo at 7 weeks of age, 1⅕in (3cm) long. The limb buds and the retina of the eyes are formed. The large dark mass in the body is the liver.

At 4 months, this human fetus could perhaps survive in an incubator. The arms and hands are more fully formed than the legs and feet, but the eyelids have not developed. Here, the umbilical cord, the embryo's lifeline, is visible behind the hands.

Baby alligators hatching from their eggs. Like most reptiles, all birds, and a few mammals, the young develop in shelled eggs from which they must break free.

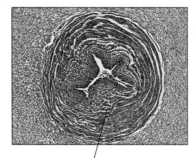

Section through the 28-in (70-cm)-long umbilical cord with, in the center, the muscular walls and passageway of the artery taking blood to the fetus.

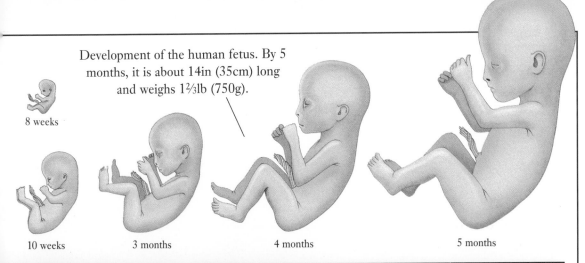

Development of the human fetus. By 5 months, it is about 14in (35cm) long and weighs 1⅔lb (750g).

8 weeks

10 weeks

3 months

4 months

5 months

FACT FILE

❏ Human development from the fertilized ovum to a newborn baby involves only 34 repeated cell divisions.

❏ The germination period of seeds is the plant equivalent of pregnancy.

❏ In the early stages of embryo development, all mammals – in fact, all vertebrates – look similar. It is only as organs become fully formed and limbs appear that major differences are apparent. It is at this stage that the mammal embryo is called a fetus. We reach this stage at about 8 weeks following fertilization, when we are no more than 1½in (3.75mm) long and weigh less than an ounce (27g).

❏ In humans, the ratio of males to females at fertilization may be up to 170 to 100 but more male embryos die during pregnancy. At birth the ratio is between 113 to 100 and 101 to 100 depending on location in the world, time of year, and standards of medical care.

❏ The longest human pregnancy on record is about 15 months and the shortest about 5½ months. Nine months – 266 days – is the average, but as there are no immediate signs, signals, or symptoms of fertilization taking place, calculating precise lengths is practically impossible.

Growth – getting bigger, becoming mature

A female Indian tiger with her 4-week-old cubs. The cubs will be dependent on their mother for food, toiletry, and protection until about 2 months old.

Living things show a varied pattern with regard to the speed of growth of the embryo, development of the newborn, and maturity of the adult. For example, the fertilized egg of a Blue whale, the largest creature on Earth, is barely visible to the unaided eye. Eleven months later, the new born Blue whale emerges, measuring 28ft (8.4m) in length and weighing 3 tons (2.7 tonnes). But it will be another 10 years or so before the youngster can mate and produce offspring. Even after maturity, the whale will continue to grow. Blue whales can live to 95 years of age and produce young every 3 or 4 years. In the plant world, some bamboos grow at 3ft (90cm) a day and live for 100 years. Then, without any apparent stimulus, they suddenly flower, set seed and, after a few days, die. Other bamboos grow no more than an inch (2.5cm) tall and live for only 2 or 3 years. We develop sexually at about 12 to 16 years of age. We continue to grow in height until we are about 18 to 20. Our brains are fully grown by the time we reach age 10 or 11, but our mental abilities continue to increase until we are well into adulthood.

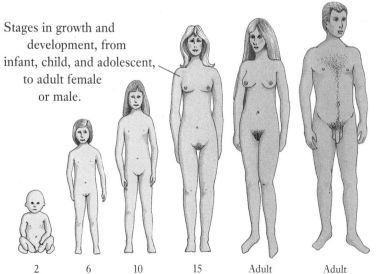

Stages in growth and development, from infant, child, and adolescent, to adult female or male.

| 2 | 6 | 10 | 15 | Adult | Adult |

A baby kangaroo in its mother's pouch. Kangaroos are marsupials – the young are born at an early stage and grow within the pouch.

Nestling Song thrushes, their mouths agape waiting for food brought to the nest by one of the parents. The young stay in the nest until able to fly – at about 12 to 16 days old.

Giant sequoias. Growing to a height of 265ft (80m) and a girth of 83ft (25m), they are the most massive of all living species. Some are around 3,500 years old.

❏ The female Nile crocodile lays between 30 and 40 eggs in a riverside nest. Both she and her male partner incubate the eggs and the young hatch 90 days later. If the eggs have been kept especially warm, males develop, and if they are kept cool, females grow. In this way, the adults can control the balance of the sexes in the population. At birth the young are about 12in (30cm) long. The female carries them in her mouth to nursery pools, where she looks after them for 8 to 10 weeks.

❏ Certain lichens growing in the frozen wastes of Alaska are more than 9,000 years old. They grow on rocks and increase in size less than 1/8th of an inch (3mm) in 100 years.

❏ Parental care is common not only among mammals but also leeches, wolf spiders, digger wasps, seahorses, frogs, birds, alligators, and pythons.

❏ The pituitary gland produces hormones stimulating the testicles or the ovaries to secrete the male hormone testosterone and the female hormones estrogen and progesterone. These chemical messengers direct the final development of our sex organs and prompt changes to our voices and to the spread of body hair. An imbalance of these hormones sometimes occurs, producing females with lots of body hair and males with pairs of breasts.

Life cycles

Chrysalis of the Monarch butterfly. This is the second stage in the insect's life cycle. The first stage, the larva or caterpillar, is a feeding machine. Within the chrysalis, or pupa, this transforms into the winged adult.

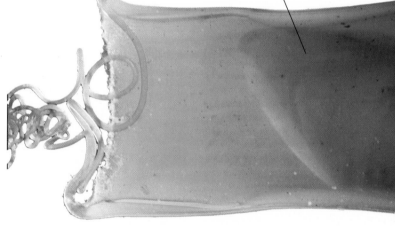

A wooden barn, neglected and abandoned to the elements, soon falls into disrepair. Rain and snow rot the wood, and wind rips the roof and walls apart.

Dogfish embryos developing within their hard, horny protective cases, 'mermaid's purses.' Related sharks produce live young, as we do.

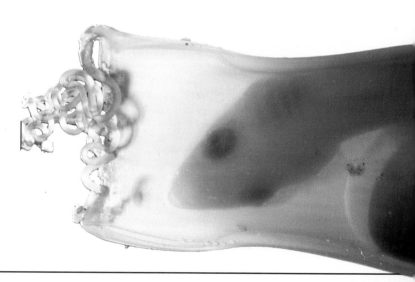

Everything that is born eventually dies. Death may result from injury, illness, or aging. Just as machines in time develop faults and cease functioning, so living things inevitably age. Aging may result from hormonal changes, a build up of wastes within cells, mutations, or a self-destruction of cells. 'Life cycle' is the term biologists use to define the various stages through which an organism passes during its lifetime. Our own life cycle is straightforward: fertilized egg to newborn to adult. Our offspring look like miniature versions of ourselves. A frog's life cycle is more complex. It involves a larval (tadpole) stage before reaching adulthood. A butterfly's life cycle has yet one more stage, the pupa or chrysalis. In the inanimate world, things do not physically change unless an outside force acts upon them. Often, we are the source of this force. Throughout this book we have looked at the parallels between ourselves, other living things, and the machines we have created. We have also touched on the influences and impact of various organisms on one another. On the following pages there are facts and figures that highlight more of these interactions and many of the plant and animal record breakers.

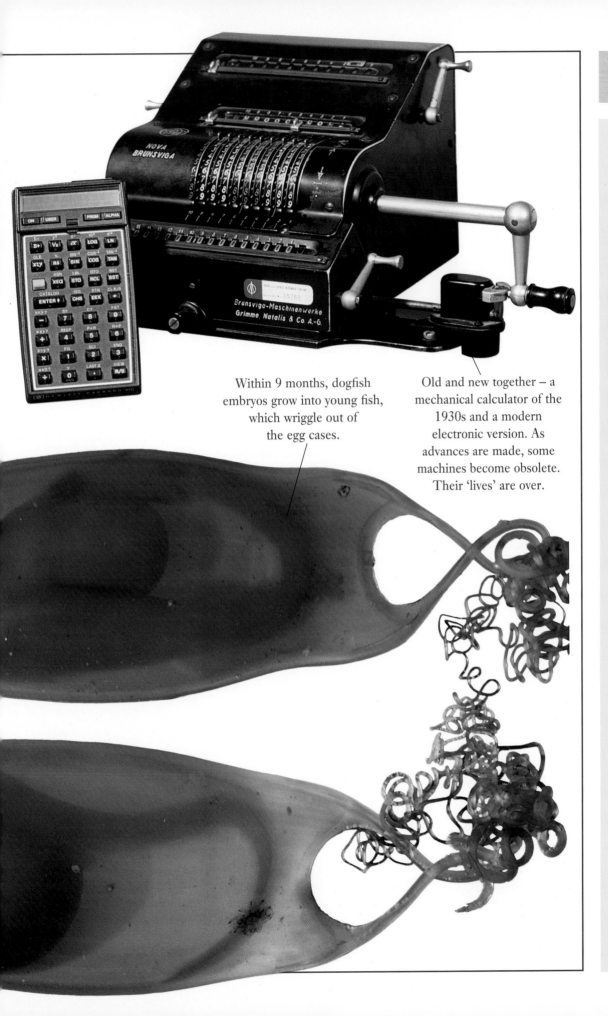

Within 9 months, dogfish embryos grow into young fish, which wriggle out of the egg cases.

Old and new together – a mechanical calculator of the 1930s and a modern electronic version. As advances are made, some machines become obsolete. Their 'lives' are over.

SUPERFACTS

Composition of the body
Water makes up just over 60 percent of an adult's body. That's about 10 gallons (38 liters), enough to fill 5 buckets. Major chemical elements in the body include hydrogen, oxygen, nitrogen, carbon, calcium, magnesium, sodium, potassium, chlorine, sulfur, and iron. The amount of carbon in the human body is enough to fill about 9,000 lead pencils.

The make-up of blood ▶
The average amount of blood in the human body is just over a gallon. Of this, plasma, a clear, straw-colored liquid, makes up 55 percent. The rest is mostly red and white blood cells. The body produces red blood cells at an average rate of 9,000 million per hour.

A hairy skin
All mammals have hairy skin on the body, including whales and seals. On a human's body there are about 1 to 2 million hairs, with about 100,000 of these growing on the scalp. Each hair on the head grows up to 1/3in (8mm) in length per month, growing for about 3 years before being replaced by another. ▼

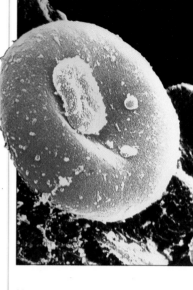

Holding one's breath
Turtles and whales can stay underwater for several hours before having to surface for air. Birds such as penguins and ducks can stay submerged for up to 15 minutes. We cannot hold our breath under water for more than about 2 minutes. The record depth for a breath-held dive is 351ft (107m) by the Italian, Angela Bandini.

Unusual bodies
Among the unusual characteristics of people are individuals who have been born with or developed: 14 fingers and 15 toes; hair more than 20ft (6.1m) in length; four sets of teeth; a brain weighing more than 4½lb (2kg).

The largest land mammal
Baluchitherium, a hornless ancestor of the rhinoceros that lived in Asia about 40 million years ago, measured about 27ft (8.23m) in length and stood 17ft (5.18m) high at the shoulders. Its bulk was about twice that of an adult elephant. The fossil bones of this extinct animal were first discovered in Baluchistan in the early part of the 20th century.

The tallest creature

The tallest living land animal is the giraffe, growing up to 20ft (6.1m) high including its horns. The tallest tree is a eucalyptus from Australia, which grows over 470ft high (143m). Haji Channa of Pakistan, at 7ft 8in (2.34m), is the tallest person alive. But there have been at least 10 men and 1 woman who have grown to more than 8ft (2.44m) tall.

▼

The heaviest animal

The most massive animal ever was the dinosaur *Brachiosaurus*. A museum specimen made up from several partial skeletons measures over 72ft (21.95m) in length, 46ft (14m) tall and weighs 33 tons (30 tonnes). But there is evidence that *Brachiosaurus* may have grown even larger, to a weight of 88 tons (80 tonnes), and another dinosaur named '*Ultrasaurus*' reached 115ft (35m) long, 56ft (17m) tall, and weighed 154 tons (140 tonnes). The largest living animal is the Blue whale, which grows to 110ft (33.5m) long and weighs more than 190 tons, (172 tonnes). The world's heaviest person was an American, Jon Minnoch, 1941-1983, who reached a weight of nearly 1,400lb (635kg).

Giants of the deep ▶

Among marine creatures there are jellyfish 6ft (1.8m) in diameter with tentacles 120ft (36.6m) in length; octopuses up to 32ft (9.7m) long from one tentacle tip to another; a squid with a tentacle span of over 65ft (19.8m) ; a clam 4ft (1.2m) across and weighing 500lb (227kg) ; and a crab with a limb span of 10ft (3m).

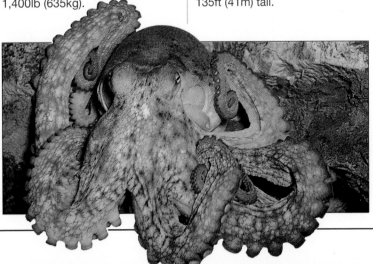

The most massive plant ▲

A Giant sequoia tree in California, U.S.A., measures 275ft (83.8m) tall and its girth – the distance round the thickest part of the trunk – is 83ft (25.3m). A cypress tree in Mexico has the greatest girth, at 117ft (35.7m), but is only 135ft (41m) tall.

Largest leaves

The Raffia palm of the Mascarene Islands in the Indian Ocean has the longest leaves – up to 78ft (23.8m) including leafstalk – while the leaves of the Water lily are the largest in diameter – more than 8ft (2.4m) across.

The largest fungus

A Puffball, a white rounded fungus found in pastures and woodlands, grows to more than 20in (50cm) in diameter. The largest specimen, found in Ohio, U.S.A., in 1988, had a circumference of 77in (196cm). The previous record holder, found in New York State in 1877, was at first mistaken for a sheep at a distance.

SUPERFACTS

Meat-eating plants
The special hollow leaves, or pitchers, in which some carnivorous plants catch animals to eat, measure up to 12in (30cm) or more in depth, while the traps of meat-eating plants such as bladderworts are smaller than a pinhead. The victims of pitcher plants – flies, spiders, scorpions, and lizards – drown in a pool of liquid trapped in the leaves, whereas bladderworts trap water fleas and other tiny animals in hollow pouches each with a trapdoor and touch-sensitive hairs around this. ▼

The largest wingspan
Quetzalcoatlus, a flying reptile that lived 70 million years ago, had a wingspan of up to 39ft (12m). The largest wingspan of any living animal is that of the Wandering albatross. It averages almost 10ft (3.2m), but is reported to reach over 13ft (4m). Bats have wingspans of up to 6ft (1.8m), and butterflies up to 11in (28cm). The aircraft with the largest wingspan was an American experimental plane, the Hughes H4 Hercules flying boat built in 1947. The span was almost 320ft (97m).

Body temperatures
Our own normal body temperature is about 98.5°F (37°C). A bird, the Western pewee of North America, has the highest body temperature, at 112.6°F (44.8°C), and frogs and salamanders have the lowest, down to 50°F (10°C).

Body plumbing and wiring
There are about 60,000 miles (96,500km) of blood vessels in the human body – enough to go more than twice around the Earth. A blood cell makes one circuit of the blood system in about 60 seconds. ▶

Information packs
Every cell in the human body contains enough DNA – the chemical containing a person's genetic blueprint – to stretch over a distance of about 6ft (1.8m), the height of an adult man. When the DNA is wound up inside a cell it is packed into 46 tiny cylinders, the chromosomes, which, laid end to end, would only have a total length of 1/100in (0.25mm). ▶

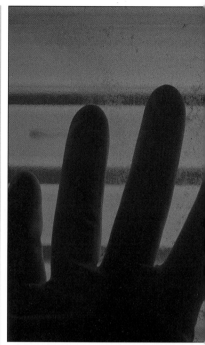

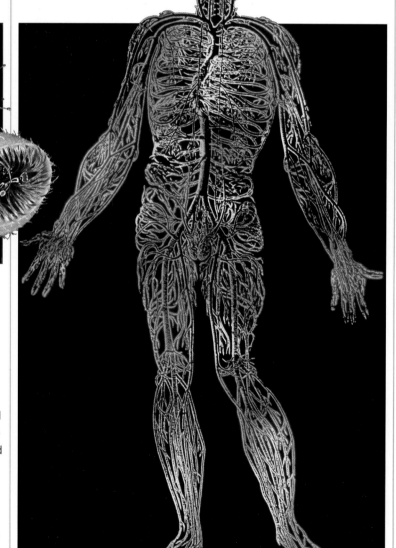

Spreading far and wide ▶
The seeds of milkweed and dandelion flowers, with their parachutes of fine white hair-like fibers, are blown by the wind many miles from the parent plant. The Squirting cucumber shoots its seeds more than 25ft (7.6m) away as it slowly fills with water then bursts. The seeds of coconut palms, enclosed within the hard, hairy nuts that get washed up on tropical beaches, are carried thousands of miles from the parent plants by the ocean currents. Seabirds carry small seeds such as those of grasses similarly long distances. As the birds wade in mud along rivers and in estuaries, seeds embedded in the mud stick to their feet. They fall or get knocked off when the birds land again.

Blood pipes
The blood vessels of a Blue whale are so large that a full-sized fish could easily swim through them. The largest blood vessel in the human body, the aorta, is about 1in (2.5cm) in diameter.

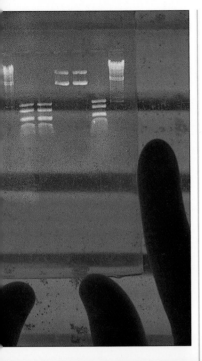

Giants of the past

Dinosaurs such as *Brachiosaurus* and *Diplodocus* weighed more than 60 tons (54 tonnes), ten times more than the African ▶ elephant, the largest land animal alive today. Other dinosaurs were quite small by comparison; *Compsognathus* was about the size of a hen and probably weighed less than 15lb (6.8kg) when fully grown. The largest marine reptile was a pliosaur that lived about 135 million years ago. Called *Kronosaurus*, it measured nearly 50ft (15.2m) in length.

Speed of evolution

It takes at least 300,000 generations for a new species to evolve from an existing one. For mammals, which take years to reach maturity, this can take more than 1 million years, but for many microbes, which can reproduce every hour or two, it may happen once every 6 months.

The big squeeze

Pythons, boas, and anacondas, the largest of all snakes, kill their victims by squeezing them to death. Then they eat their meals whole. These snakes wrap themselves around prey then constrict – tighten their grip by contracting their muscles – until the victims suffocate.

Fossil records

The earliest evidence of life on Earth is a 3,200 million-year-old fossil bacterium. The oldest animal and plant fossils date from about 600 million years ago. Some of the most dramatic fossils are dinosaur footprints, preserved in mud for over 80 million years, each print measuring over 3ft (0.9m) long. The oldest fossil human is a young woman who has been nicknamed Lucy. She lived in East Africa about 3 million years ago.

Sharp vision ▶

Insects can see movement that takes place in as little as one-thousandth of a second. They can easily see a light bulb flashing on and off 50 times a second

The biggest eyes

The largest animal eyes are those of the Giant squid. Each measures 16in (41cm) across and contains more than 1,000 million light-sensitive cells. These cannot distinguish colors, though. A squid sees only in monochrome.

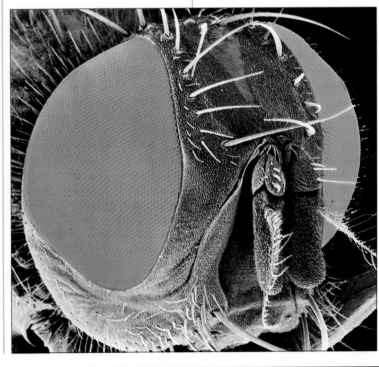

SUPERFACTS

Living without water

An average adult needs more than 3 pints (1.7 liters) of water a day, not necessarily to drink, but as a component of all foodstuffs. Without water people die in 3 to 4 days, but can live for several weeks without food. An Arabian (one-humped) camel can live without water for up to 10 months, cautiously using up whatever its body contains. Its hump stores food in the form of fat and is not a water store, as is popularly imagined.

The most legs

Millipedes have upwards of 200 legs, with the record being 750. Centipedes have between 28 and 354 legs. (Millipedes appear to have two pairs of legs per body segment instead of the centipedes' one, but each segment of present-day millipedes evolved from the joining together of segments in earlier types.) Next come Velvet worms, with up to 82 legs. Starfish and their relatives are usually thought of as having 5 legs (or arms), but some have up to 50. ▼

Length of pregnancy

The longest period from fertilization of an egg to birth or hatching is that of the Indian elephant at an average of 624 days. Next is the rhinoceros at 560 days. The longest incubation period for birds is 79 days, for the Royal albatross. The average human pregancy lasts 265 days.

Microlife ▶

Most viruses, bacteria, yeasts, and the spores of many types of simple plants and animals are too small to be seen with the naked eye. Many tens or hundreds of thousands of viruses could sit on the period at the end of this sentence. Bacteria are on average 10 to 100 times larger than viruses, but few are larger than our own red blood cells – of which there are more than 5 million in each drop of blood.

Four-minute warning

Every cell in the body needs oxygen and without it each will die in only 4 minutes. Oxygen helps change food into chemical energy needed by cells for their internal chemistry.

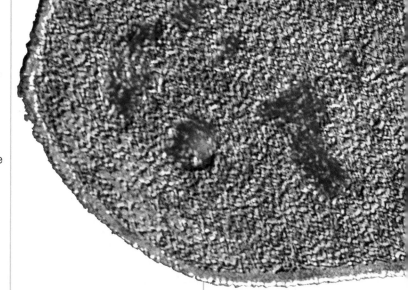

Lifetime of cells

Human skin cells last about 6 or 7 days before they die. Red blood cells have a lifespan of about 4 months, and bone cells live for between 10 and 30 years.

Laid out flat

If an adult person's skin was laid out flat, it would cover an area of about 22 square feet (2m²).

The digestive tract

Our digestive system or tract – often known as the alimentary canal – includes a tube more than 30ft (9m) long extending from the mouth to the anus. The longest component part of the tube is the small intestine. This measures about 21ft (6.5m) in length and about 1in (2.5cm) in diameter. It is tightly folded up within the belly part of the body – forming our 'guts.' From the time food enters the mouth, it takes only a few minutes to reach the small intestine but here it remains for several hours to be digested. Complete digestion of a meal takes about 24 hours.

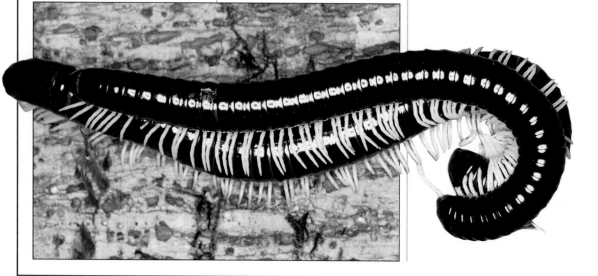

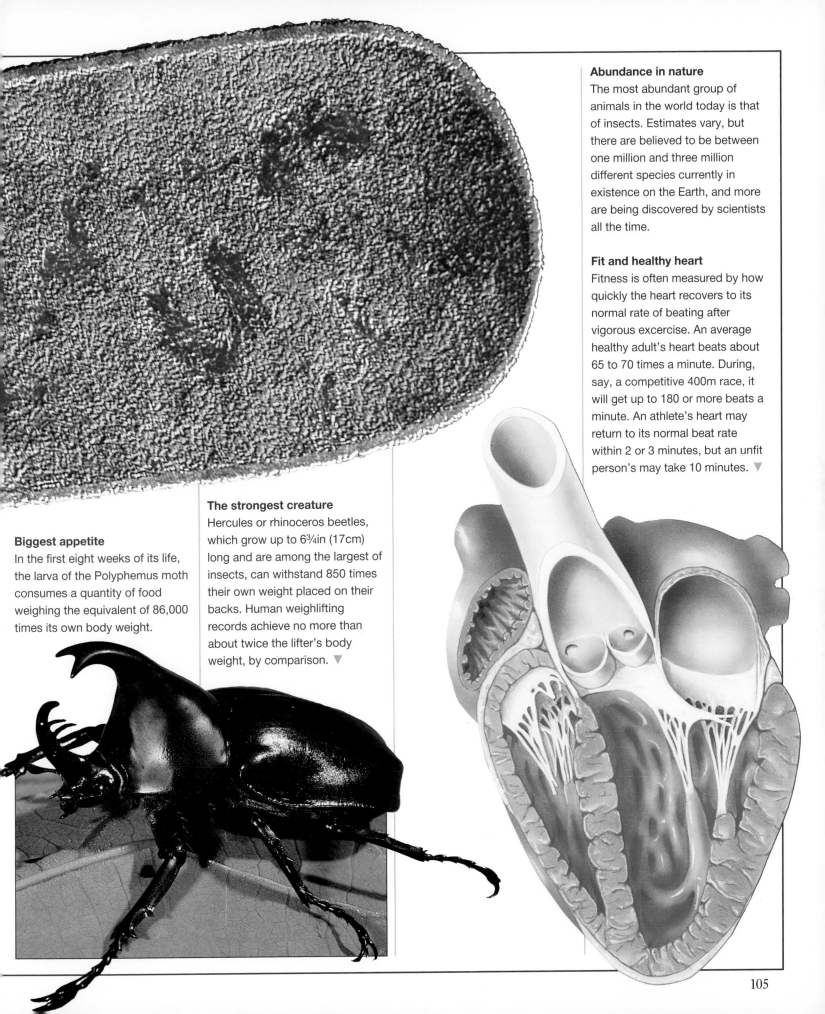

Abundance in nature

The most abundant group of animals in the world today is that of insects. Estimates vary, but there are believed to be between one million and three million different species currently in existence on the Earth, and more are being discovered by scientists all the time.

Fit and healthy heart

Fitness is often measured by how quickly the heart recovers to its normal rate of beating after vigorous excercise. An average healthy adult's heart beats about 65 to 70 times a minute. During, say, a competitive 400m race, it will get up to 180 or more beats a minute. An athlete's heart may return to its normal beat rate within 2 or 3 minutes, but an unfit person's may take 10 minutes. ▼

The strongest creature

Hercules or rhinoceros beetles, which grow up to 6¾in (17cm) long and are among the largest of insects, can withstand 850 times their own weight placed on their backs. Human weighlifting records achieve no more than about twice the lifter's body weight, by comparison. ▼

Biggest appetite

In the first eight weeks of its life, the larva of the Polyphemus moth consumes a quantity of food weighing the equivalent of 86,000 times its own body weight.

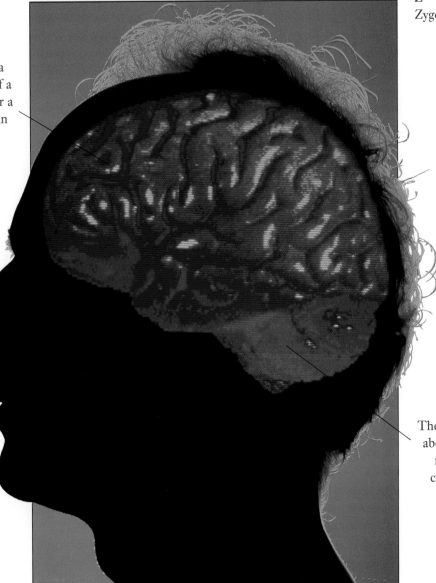

A composite image showing a computer-generated picture of a man's brain superimposed over a photograph of his head seen in profile view.

The brain of a male adult weighs about 3lb (1.4kg), and contains more than 10 billion nerve cells. It is linked to the body by the spinal cord.

PICTURE CREDITS

The publishers wish to thank the following agencies who have supplied photographs for this book. The photographs have been credited by page number and, where necessary, by position on the page: (B)Bottom, T(Top), L(Left), BR(Bottom Right), etc.

A false-color photograph of a section through a human brain.

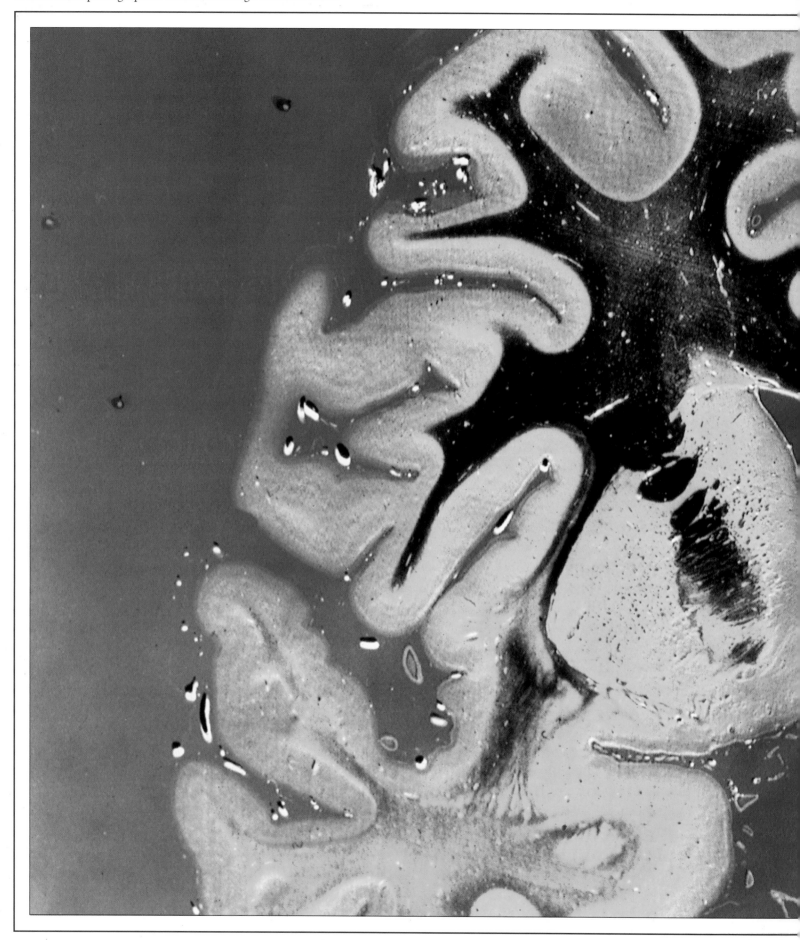